T0193859

ANNA'S
CHRISTMAS

ANNA'S
CHRISTMAS

HIDDEN TRUTH POEMS

CHERYL FREIER

authorHOUSE®

AuthorHouse™
1663 Liberty Drive
Bloomington, IN 47403
www.authorhouse.com
Phone: 1 (800) 839-8640

Published by AuthorHouse 08/28/2015

ISBN: 978-1-5049-3361-2 (sc)
ISBN: 978-1-5049-3362-9 (e)

Library of Congress Control Number: 2015913784

Print information available on the last page.

*Any people depicted in stock imagery provided by Thinkstock are models,
and such images are being used for illustrative purposes only.
Certain stock imagery © Thinkstock.*

This book is printed on acid-free paper.

*Because of the dynamic nature of the Internet, any web addresses or
links contained in this book may have changed since publication and
may no longer be valid. The views expressed in this work are solely those
of the author and do not necessarily reflect the views of the publisher,
and the publisher hereby disclaims any responsibility for them.*

Contents

Dedication for the Book Anna's Christmas Hidden Truth Poems

This book is dedicated to the man that I was married to, Martin Freier. He was an exceptional person in every way. He was able to turn the evil that he experienced as a young boy in Nazi Slovakia into good and into a life of goodness and dedication to helping people. I will miss Martin always. He was my inspiration. He recognized my talent for writing. He helped me to pursue my talent for writing. I will always be indebted to him for his goodness and thoughtfulness.

A short rendition of some of the poems that Martin wrote:

Life and the Clock

Life is like a clock.
It keeps ticking away
Tick tock, tick tock
Every single day,
Today, as it did yesterday.
Sometimes life appears too slow,
Sometimes much too fast.
Now as in the past.
Life's rhythm is steady
Whether or not we're ready.

On and on life goes
Without skipping a beat,
Sometimes helping us to forget
Our woes,
The bitter cold and the heat
When we're jubilant or beat.
We lose count
Of the passing hours,
Too busy to smell the flowers.
Sometimes there is sun;
Sometimes only showers.
There are four seasons
'cause G-d has His reasons.
And our heart goes ting-a-ling.
Winter follows autumn in full force.
And time runs its course.
Then suddenly we look around
And snow covers the ground.
As life keeps rolling on,
Another year has gone.
Wish life would pause to give
Us a chance.
For one more glance,
Just one more dance.
Sooner or later we're bound to ask:
"Whatever happened to all those years:
the laughter and the tears?"
Few ever get a real taste of it.
Some manage to make a mess or it.
Oh what a waste!
Too many precious moments pass by,

Without people asking why.
When they look around,
The day is gone.
Tomorrow comes on the wings
Of a bird that sings.
No way to bring yesterdays
Back agtain;
Be it joy or pain.
Oh yes, we sometimes remember
That moment in July or September.
But the laughter and joy
Of a girl and boy,
Once happy on that summer beach
Is soon out of reach.
Life is like a clock.
It keeps rolling on and on,
Without a pause.
It has a beginning and the end
Iks just around the bend.
Too late do we realized
We're only part of life's game.
Here today. Gone tomorrow----
a little joy; lots of sorrow.
Life disappears
Like a summer breeze.
Sooner or later the time or reckoning
Is beckoning.
Until then keep up we must
Or we end up in the dust.

Life And The Jigsaw Puzzle

Like a jigsaw puzzle,
Life manages to befuddle
And confuse us with lots of
Unanswered questions and tensions.
Clues are everywhere,
But reveal few answers.
Little wonder we get that
Feeling of hanging in mid-air,
Crying that life isn't fair.
We keep on searching for the missing pieces,
Hoping to find peace of mind.
Just when we think we have found all there is,
Ready to have a ball,
Some of our pieces just tumble and fall.
That's when we realize
That only by learning the name of the game
Can we lay claim to paradise.

Wondering

Wondering why the sun in the sky
Makes each day a new day.
Why do the moon and stars
light up the sky for us at night?
I keep wondering why
In all this beauty and plenty
There's still no Justice and Liberty.
Why is there so much
Inhumanity?
Too many of our brethen are ill fed,
Just left in the gutter for dead.

Is there a need to question
Your neighbor's creed,
While the innocent bleed?
Amid this God's creation of wonder,
We allow wars and plunder
And missiles that kill with thunder.
I keep wondering
Whether mankind will ever unite
In a common cause that is right
So that children can sleep at night.
Will there ever be an end to strife
And the taking of innocent life?

Greed
Like a weed, greed spreads its seed.
Its appetite grows without end in sight.
Why this is so nobody knows.
Lodged deep within some men and women,
It is a craving, an urge for more,
Again and again.
Whether there's sunshine or rain,
Man's thirst for more
Cannot be quenched.
With the finest champagne,
This hunter cannot be filled.
The need for more money,
For more gold and diamonds
Will always remain,
Though it drives man insane.
No matter how sweet,
His life is never complete.

Everything's chewed to its core,
Until the cup once full has run
Dry and there's no more.

Hate

Like a brush fire
That never ends, 'hate' just spreads
Throughout the neighborhood,
Though it does little good.
In its wake, hate keeps burning,
Always churning,
And using everything that is good
For fodder and food.
Fanned by the winds from the Northeast,
Hate breeds hate
Among those that are blessed
And those that are cursed by fate.
When people are fighting
In its presence,
hate is winning,
By piling lies upon lies
While love is dying,
No one who is in its path
Can escape hate's wrath.
It sets friend against friend
Until it achieves its malicious end.

The many powerful well-written poems by Martin Freier
can be found in the book, The Day Of The Hidden Truth
Poems.

Introduction

Anna's Christmas

Hidden Truth Poems.

Cheryl Freier

From the prayer book: "Favor me O Lord and I shall move mountains".

Understanding what happened during the Holocaust is one of the most powerful thoughts to understand and remains one of those complicated conundrums, and dark mysteries in all of the history of the world. It is a traverse into a mystery realm of circumstances that never existed before. In historical and human context as well, it remains one of the darkest times of human history, an overt and intentional expression of vulgarity of the lead people; it was in all essence, the devaluing of the value and sanctity of human life. It remains one of the darkest times in human history that no one can excuse. The massive following of wrong and wanton ideas set civilization back hundreds and hundreds of years. Laws of people's basic rights of freedoms were disregarded and abandoned. Massive panic created pandemonium. All this wrong was created in the mind of one person initially. People were not confident or schooled enough in the right values and naively followed this wanton killer, Hitler, and his bandit entourage. It was a tragedy of epic proportions that followed. It was never seen in history before and hopefully will never be allowed to happen in history again.

WWII was a war to end all wars. It was a war to end freedom in the countries of Europe. It was a war designed to conquer all countries in the world. A mad man caused all this. What was his purpose? His purpose was to become king of the world. His plans were to create a world in which there was a utopia only for him and for those whom he chose to join him. He wanted to annihilate a people, the Hebrews. It was only time before he would plan to annihilate other peoples. He wanted to recreate animals that had become extinct. He was fascinated by bringing back the 'so-called dead'. He wanted a world that he had chosen to create that he was the master of. Hitler planned to become a Lord of a castle. Hitler wanted to recreate a feudal society in which he was the king, the supreme ruler of all of the peoples and ruler of all of the animals in the world. Hitler almost succeeded. Thus, had Hitler succeeded in his wanton desires, civilization and all of the values for life and living in a lawful way would have been turned back for at least six hundred years. All of the advances that had been made to improve mankind throughout the centuries would have been forgotten.

My mother-in-law, Anna Freier, and her family were caught in the throes of the war in Nazi occupied Slovakia. It was difficult to survive most of the war years. The family lived in Micholovce, Slovakia and their town bordered near Russia on the top, and bordered two other European countries near its sides. Many of the citizens of Slovakia had the advantage of a location that was distant and hard to get to, but the Nazis were still there, but not in full force. The Nazis were not in full force in the summer of 1944, when the Slovak military forces returned from England to Nazi-driven Slovakia to drive the Nazis out of their country. Thus, the battlefields came to the soils, and mountains, and plains of Slovakia, and to the cites, and to the towns. It became the hardest time to survive the war. The Germans were out to kill any Jew or other person who opposed them.

The Germans grew to be fearful of losing the war, and they resorted to drafting young boys to fill their ranks of fighting soldiers. This was one of the many extreme measures that they took to win the war. The Nazi rationale was kill, kill, and then kill again. There was no reasoning behind their psychotic impulses. Their thoughts were based on animal behavior.

In all over the world in this dark time in human history, leaders did not know how to stop the wanton killing and the persecution of innocent people. As was mentioned, the real reasons why the Holocaust took place have been a major issue of debate since the war ended in May of 1945. The biggest question remains, however; given the same set of circumstances, would the Holocaust happen again? Perhaps it would happen again. We must continue to write about the Holocaust. If one writes the stories of what happened in the Holocaust, people will become permanently imbued and aware of all of the many hardships in surviving a war that was meant to end all wars.

The question one should ask is how did people, the Jews survive this war when the ultimate plan of the Nazis was to annihilate this people who have been in existence since before the birth of Christ? The answer to this question has many parts to the answers. It is certain that there were 135,000 Jews living in Slovakia before the war. After the war, there were only 25,000 Jews remaining. It was a miracle that these 25,000 Jews survived.

One of the partisan groups which was formed in Slovakia was the Working Group Party. Key members of this Slovakian group were Gisi Fleischmann and Rabbi Michael Ber Weismandl. Rabbi Weismandl was the head of the Yeshiva in Nitra, Slovakia. Nitra was the fourth largest city in Slovakia at the time. The Working Group was responsible for bribing Slovakian officials, and Nazi officers, and paid ransom to key Nazi officials. As a result of their efforts, the deportation and selection of Jews for transport to Auschwitz was delayed from 1942 until 1944. Many Jews were spared as a result.

It is certain that the Jews were helped by Christians. There were Christians who risked their lives to help the Jews to survive. The bravery of those Christians shall forever be remembered by survivors. The bravery of these Christian people will be forever remembered in the annals of the history of people, the history of this world war, in the historical annals of Christian history, and in the historical annals of Hebrew history, and in the history of those who live in the sky above us, the angels.

This story, Anna's Christmas, is a story of survival against enormous odds. It is a special story that shows courage and faith beyond almost human endurance. This is Anna Freier's story. It is her story about the miracle that happened to save her and her family from starvation on the night before the Christmas holiday. Anna and her family were starving in a bunker, which was built below the ground in the woods near the mountains of Slovakia. There was virtually no hope for the family's survival, but Anna continued to pray for the safety and survival of her family. This is Anna's story! It is the month of December. It is the year 1944.

Anna's story is based on a true-to-life story. It must be told to generations and generations of people. We must, therefore as writers write continuously on the Holocaust subject and include the historical analysis and results. We must tell all we know about what happened. We must delve, yes, into the historical issues which were involved, but we must delve into the religious and spiritual issues that were involved, too. In World War II, the basic covenant with G-d, the understanding and the following of the two tablets that G-d handed down to Moses on Mount Sinai. The aggressor's side, the Nazism was the following of the devil and doing its wrong deeds. The angels represented all peoples of all creeds, and nationalities, and religions. There were angels in WWII who helped the innocent victims and the downtrodden. Of This I am most certain. The angels helped as many people who were good people as they could. The angels helped those Nazis that were capable of redemption. There were too few angels to go around.

The light of day comes forth for all peoples all over the world at daybreak. The eternal light, however, shines forever and always for all people who follow the two tablets of law that were passed down to Moses to give to the people to follow and to live their lives by this code. The eternal light will shine within those who follow this covenant with G-d. Eternal life will follow for those who walk in the pathways of righteousness, and goodness, and follow the laws that were passed down to the people by G-d.

Anna Freier and her family were caught in the throes of the Nazi occupation of Slovakia. Up until the last months of the war in the year 1944, it was difficult to survive, and there were many times that they envisioned that they were doomed, but Anna and her family were able to return back to their home in Micholovce, Slovakia. The last year of the war from the summer of 1944 to May of 1945 were the most difficult to survive in. The winter of 1944 was the hardest to survive of all of the winters. It was a winter of fierce snow storms and unrelenting, bitter cold. For the person who hid in the woods, it was a most difficult situation to find food and to keep warm from the cold. Anna and her family survived in an underground bunker that led into a cave. During the last month of the year, December of 1944, it was almost impossible for the family to survive. The weather had turned colder than usual. There were more frequent snow storms. Ice had formed on a lot of the snow.

The Nazis were bolder in their defenses and in their offensive. They were more determined to kill off Jews and to kill off any persons who opposed them. The Nazis were imbued with hatred and were programmed to kill whoever got into their way. More Nazis than even were in the area of Micholovce. For those Nazis who did not see the light coming forth to show them a better way, they were destined to perish, however. The angels of G-d were intervening on behalf of innocent people. The angels of G-d were protecting soldiers and partisans resisting the Nazi terror. The problem was that there was not enough angels to deal with the Nazi terror. For those few Nazi soldiers who did see the light and realized that they were wrong and stopped their wrong doings, there was redemption from the tragedy of circumstances that all men, good or bad were thrown into.

What is the connection between the bright shining light of goodness and evil that was done to people in the Holocaust? The light of goodness allows us to see good in mankind and to do good for people. Otherwise we would be in complete darkness as was the state of mind of the Nazis and their terror.

Questions are asked throughout our searching history. The question: what would you do if you were caught in the throes of a deadly war that would most distinguish yourself? This is a soul-searching question that requires a most powerful answer. The idea behind the answer would have to have a good purpose. There are many answers to this question. Rescue attempts to rescue children from the throes of a Second World War were being made as soon as Hitler took power. Many families got together and put up funds to rescue the eldest child from the war. The family would send the eldest child to another country where they knew that the eldest would be safe. Reality was on the minds of many people. No one, however, dreamt that the war would last until May of 1945 and that it would take such an unbelievable toll of human lives. No one could have imagined a Holocaust with gas chambers and crematoriums, ghastly instruments of the devil Nazis.

The question, "What is it that distinguishes one man from another" is one of the most powerful, meaningful, poignant questions that is asked and especially asked during a war. The answer might be, "It is the legacy of truth and goodness that he shows during the length of the war period. That can be a powerful answer to this powerful and poignant question. We are all tested by good and bad happenings in our lives. Many times it is more of bad than good that happens during a lifetime. It is how we overcome the difficult problems and give ourselves hope to live for a better day that determines whether we will become an example for other people to follow and for others to remember. And, yes, it is how we handle success of leadership and do good actions with the power of leadership that determines whether we will be remembered as a famous person who contributed in a good way to people. Otherwise, by doing bad deeds with the power of leadership, it is a defined destiny that one will be remembered in infamy. Hitler will be remembered in infamy.

It Is The Individual Who Prevails
Throughout History

Throughout the centuries, historians have recorded information on people who were leaders. Historians have recorded what has happened to people, and cities, and the topography that was around them. There are many who would say that G-d has recorded the history of these leaders, too. These stories are always fascinating to read, because one is always interested in how people lived and survived in centuries before their time. The stories reveal the weaknesses and the strengths of people in good times and in times of peril, too. The stories of history reveal how social dynamics determines to a large extent the individual's lot in life. Conversely, history reveals the triumphs, and revelations, and determinations of individuals, and the discoveries that people made facing the odds. When all is told, however, it is the name of the individual that prevails most in history. Abraham became the father of two nations. Christ founded Christianity. And the list goes on and on to include Einstein and his theory of relativity, a discovery that changed the scientific way matter in the atmosphere became viewed. Dr. Salk finding the polio virus saved the lives of hundreds and hundreds of thousands of young children and adults. Armstrong ventured to explore the moon and the whole exploration, and discovery of planets, and minerals in outer space changed. There were many other notable persons who have achieved notable distinctions.

❄   ❄   ❄

History Is The Storyteller Of Truths

History is a virtual synthesizer of facts from happenings. History is the actual record of what happened in every moment of our time. History tells the truth. History is like hidden truth poems, which tell the story in poetic words and form, but nevertheless tells the truth. History sifts out the truth, and tells the truth, and essence into a series of poems. History vindicates the good and exposes the bad even when the good were punished wrongfully.

❄   ❄   ❄

The Bible Is A Spiritual Content

The Bible is a book for spiritual reading and prayer, but it is also an historical account of what happened to people centuries in the past. The Bible is one of the earliest recordings of history. Because of the recordings of the Bible, we know about the people who were the forefathers of our generations and so, therefore, there is a heritage for mankind to appreciate. A heritage to believe in is important for it helps one to believe in oneself.

❀　❀　❀

Of History And People And Heroes

What is history if you do not have people to tell the story? Hitler wanted to eradicate an entire population of people, and he almost succeeded. What saved the Jews who survived was the beneficent assistance of Christian believers who were willing to risk their lives, because they knew that the Nazis were evil and were doing wrong. These men and women who knew the difference between right and wrong and were willing to do the right thing were also the heroes of WWII. What saved the Jews in the end of the war was the relentless pursuit of the Nazi soldiers by General Patton and his extremely well-trained soldiers. These soldiers were the heroes of WWII, too. What saved the Jews, too, was their unwillingness to die at the hands of a maniac who was deranged. Another group of unsung heroes of WWII were those men and women who escaped into the woods and to the mountains near the towns that they lived in and struggled every day with existence. Faith kept these people alive for they believed in their G-d. They believed in themselves, and they knew that by surviving the war that they would become the ultimate winners.

❋   ❋   ❋

The War In Europe Was A War To End All Wars

The war in Europe was a war to end all wars. Contrived by men who were driven by greed and by women who thought they were the embodiment of sexuality and wit, they sought to kill anyone who did not fit their image. But the truth was that they were driven by an uncontrollable rage. The rage was deeply set within them. The rage had no boundaries, and had to be stopped. The rage had to be stopped by a force that was stronger than they were. It had to be stopped by the hand of the almighty G-d and ultimately it was. It was the historical reality that this time period will go down in infamy as no other period in history. Hatched as a nefarious plot to eliminate any one and anything that stood in their way, they succeeded in overturning governments in Europe by lies and psychotic wit.

The innocent suffered worse than anyone else. Children died from disease and hunger by the thousands. Young people who were at the prime of their lives died from hunger, and disease, and from deprivation. The Nazi scourge was too brutal. Without the intervention of American armies fighting across all of Europe, and the relentless Russian armies, the Nazis would have won the war. As the evil Nazis were defeated, one can view historical fact in all truth as the evolving of man's ability to promote peace and welfare for the whole world. Indeed, we have had within our century, many men of distinction who pursued peace and their endeavors achieved fruition. Pope John Paul was one man who had a giant capacity to free the world of the evil pestilence, the Nazis.

The Freier Family Was Caught In The Throes Of the War

Anna Freier was caught in the throes of the power hungry mongrels. She had had a good life with her husband and her family. Her everyday routines were pretty much mapped out. My mother-in-law and her family had many harrowing escapes during the war. The first book that I wrote, <u>The Grayling: Hidden Truth Poems</u> wrote about the family's experiences in eluding capture from the German soldiers during the early part of the war when the Germans soldiers marched into Slovakia. The fifth novel, <u>Echoes Resounding from The Past: Hidden Truth Poems</u> is a powerful composite of stories about war heroes. The book ends with the story being told about Anna's four sons. The boys were brought to a farm nearby to Micholovce to hide in a hidden room that was built in the back of a barn. The boys did escape from the Germans, but there were at least two narrow, harrowing escapes. I promise you will have the sense of wonder and appreciation for the freedom that we have in this country, when you finish reading the book.

The Change in All Life Activities because of the War

It was now in the late part of the summer of 1944. The family had fled into the woods. The Slovak armies had returned to Slovakia to wage war against the Nazis and take back their country. This time the fear that Anna had for herself and her family was worse than ever. Their fears were justified, especially since the armies of Hitler invaded Hungary in this last year of the war and the Nazis were more brutal than ever.

Anna, and Joseph, and the children knew that the Nazis had come to kill all of the Jews that were left in the country for what the Nazis called "the final solution". They knew that the Nazis wanted to kill off all of the Jews before the war ended and that they were determined to do so. The Nazis at this time were struggling to overcome their recent battle losses. The recent victories of the Americans, and British, and French against them enraged them. They would not be quieted. They were acting from psychotic impulses and delusions. The Nazis were powered by the physical strength of panthers. They acted and thought like the wild panthers and leopards. Can a panther stop itself from pursuing its designated prey? No it cannot. Is the victim of the panther doomed? Yes. It most certainly is doomed. How can a panther be stopped? A panther or a leopard can only be stopped by killing them off. The Jews who were hiding in the forest knew that the Nazis could come to kill them at any moment. They lived with this fear and it bit into them, gnawing and gnawing as though a poison was taking over their internal systems. The fear encompassed their minds. When the Freier family ran into hiding this time into the woods near Micholovce, they knew that it was either escape to the woods or die instantly. The Germans found those people who were left in the town who were Jews, and they marched them immediately into the fetid smelling odors of the impossibly crowded trains. The trains took them into the gates of a land built for the extermination of Jews.

❊　❊　❊

Outside in the Raw Cold Weather in the Wilderness in Nazi Slovakia

Outside in the raw cold weather in the wilderness in Slovakia, there was silence. There was a complete silence from the voices of people. It was only the sounds of the birds and the sounds of lightning and thunder—it was the sounds of the outdoors that could be heard. It was as though Anna Freier and her young family were the only ones left in the world. It was a silence out there in the stillness of the day that few people experienced. Anna stood straight with her two feet steady on the earth when she was outside of the bunker. Although she seemed meek and very worn by the war, she was strong enough to wish to fight to the end. She was ready for anything.

❊　❊　❊

The Silence In The Woods Was Soothing

It was a natural silence when they were in the woods that comforted her the most. Her thoughts were invariably interrupted by the quick sound of the fast beating, pumping heart of a rabbit. Only a few minutes later, this pacing sound was interrupted by the fleeting movements of the quick-footed four legs of a rabbit. The rabbit was determined and running to a destination that only he knew where it was. This quick, fleeting, and yet gentle-tapping of the ground was interrupted by a young buck, who was taking a quick leap over a large log, which had lain dormant, decaying and almost half way dissolved into the ground.

The silence would begin again. "Maybe I am hearing the silence of the dead", Anna muttered to herself. Her thoughts rotated to wishful thinking that all of the people that she knew would be alive, as she said while she shook her head back and forth a few times, "It was almost as though the war had stopped". The silence felt soothing, but just thinking the thought of the war being over was nurturing to her growling, hungry body. Her body was almost ravenous for food. She knew that her husband and her children would need food soon, or they would die. Anna knew the realities. The war had not ended. It had intensified. The Germans had started a counteroffensive. They had taken over Hungary with the worst, fiercest fighting in the war. Their armies had come from the south of Slovakia and had swept up to the heart, and soul, and breath of every beautiful city, and every treasured city in all of the countries that were neighboring the borders of Slovakia and into Slovakia. Now, almost straight from the epic, historical city of Bratislava, the mechanical robots of hate and killing had laid siege of Micholovce, while leaving an undeniable trail of blood, and dying, and a destruction that was so desolate that it had not been paralleled throughout history.

❊ ❊ ❊

Description Of Anna's Feelings

Anna felt a feeling of tightness all around her body, particularly around her chest. Her clothing was tightly wrapped around her, because the winds were blowing from at least two directions and just for a few moments at a time, she could feel the push, pull, and force of the two winds around her. As the winds came together, they wrapped her clothing around her body. She felt surprisingly good. It was as though the winds were protecting her from the elements around her. The chill outside as well as the dampness down in the bunker had made her clothes cling to her body tightly anyway, but that was only momentary, and then they relinquished their hold.

"Ha". She smiled. She laughed for a moment. She thought the clinging was almost like young children holding on to their mother's legs, because they wanted comfort and they wanted to hold on to her forever. Her hands felt cold. She slipped her hands into her pockets. The inside lining of the pockets was soft and smooth. "No tears or holes", she remarked to herself. And she smiled as she rotated her standing from one foot to the other.

A tear formed in her left eye. Her thoughts changed from the bleakness of the terrain, as she looked at the endless stretches of trees, and bushes, and the many mountains that were within her eyes' distance. Extending her hands out to the sky, she reached, and reached while resisting the winds. She wasn't complaining. She was praying. She was praying for her family's salvation from the death and the horrors that were taking place. She knew that these were the darkest of hours.

She thought about being in the confines of her bunker, and with the chill that clung to the outside of her body, and the momentary feelings of hopelessness about her surroundings, she had hope within her heart when she prayed. She wasn't complaining, but she had to see the sky and appeal to the Highest One for help. She could no longer be silent. She had to see some hope that the war would soon come to an end.

She had come out of the bunker to feel the cold and chilling breezes of winter upon her. She wanted to feel her life pulsating and to know that she was alive, and she wanted to hear the pulsating beats of her heart. She had to see the light from the day. She had to look up into the sky, and see the sun, and feel the rays of the sun upon her. She had to know that she was alive and that she was more than alive. She had to cry out and hear her voice. She had to know that she was alive and not one of the ghosts. Hundreds and thousands of bodies had fallen. Skeletons that had fallen were spirits that were speaking and they told G-d and his angels what was happening. Some of the dead were lucky enough to be buried, and some were not. Some of the dead were her nine sisters and their families. She cried for them and breathed in and out many times to try to overcome her distraught feelings.

About her sisters and their families, their spirits escaping the fires and the gas chambers, but not their bodies. She knew their fate. They died before their time on earth was allotted to be over--that was for certain. The entire ordering and designations of life and death that was designed by G-d was disregarded. No one was left alive to say prayers over their graves. No one would ever visit their grave. Many times gravesites and the stillness of the graves were desecrated and the earth in which the coffins lay was stomped upon by the defying, churning wheels on the tanks of the Nazi soldiers. She shook her head as she thought to herself, "such blatant disregard for life and the living and the death and the dead".

Anna had to reach over and touch a fallen branch and touch a fallen leaf to feel the natural resistance as she tried to break the branch. The branch was devoid of any movement or feeling and moved in whatever direction that she pulled at it. There was no apparent life within it, and yet it existed. It was a life. It was a life of its own. The leaf stayed in the palm of her hand as though it was a butterfly that had just stopped to rest. The leaf, all brown and wilted, but aged as it should be, stayed in her hand until the winds blew it away from her. She watched the leaf blow through the air in up and down movements and then it fell when it was almost beyond eye range. She asked herself the questions, "Would she be able to blow leaves for a long, long time?" She had to prove to herself that she was alive. This helped. She breathed in and out the December cold air. She looked now through the cold, chilling air as though she was looking through a thin piece of glass that covered an empty window pane. Would she be able to survive much longer without any food? This was her question. She did not wish to become a fallen branch that lay on the ground and disintegrated slowly until it was no more.

She needed assurance that she was still alive and that this was not a bad dream. Her husband was sleeping now, but he really did not sleep any more. He had to be vigilant. He was at least resting. Her sons were sleeping now, but they really did not sleep like ordinary people. They had trained themselves that if they heard even the smallest sound, they would get up quickly. By being in the woods, they were removed from a bitter world, a world of conflagration, a world divided between those who were hunted and those who were the relentless hunters.

She had always been a strong minded person. She had helped her mother live with kidney disease. She had taken in her father when her mother passed away. He was a handful at times for he always wanted to be the boss of the whole household, and he was getting senile, and she knew that she managed her children well enough with Joseph. Still she gave him a room on the side of the kitchen, and he was warm, and he was never hungry. Joseph would buy him clothes and take him where he wanted to go.

Hiding from the Nazis had worn Anna down. She knew that she had to renew her spiritual resilience every once and a while or she would give in to inertia. She knew well the name of the game. If she gave into fear and inertia, then she would die, and her children would die, and her husband would die. She had to be like the grayling fish---fighting, fighting to the very end and never giving up and then fighting even more to stay alive. She knew the essence of survival: live life, and fight on to live life for a sustaining better day and for more hope that the war would end. By fighting she meant to fight for the eternal life vigil fight and not fighting like fighting with her fists. She knew that there were always problems in life. Now the problems with the Nazis made everyone fear for their lives. She always knew that she had to think about what was the best thing to do for her children while the war was raging. The reality was the war was raging worse than ever throughout countries in Europe, and the Nazis were stealing, and plundering, and raping, and killing, and rounding up the Jews to take them to extermination camps; she knew that happenings in the world were pretty bad. She knew to count her blessings that she and her family were still alive, but on the other hand, how could she continue to live in rags and continue to be on the verge of hunger?

What she needed now more than ever was to fight the devil itself, the Nazis with her whole inner-being— that meant her spirit, her will, her faith in her G-d, and it meant her faith in herself for she knew that she was a good person. She had to use her eyes, and her ears, and her whole spirit of being to get control over herself and the situation. What she needed was to fight against her nagging sense of fear and feelings of deprivation. The fear was impossible to deal with at times, but she knew she had to live for her children and for her husband. She could not even think about what had happened to her father, and all of her nine sisters, and their families. She remembered their faces for a flash of a minute. The picture of their faces flashed in front of her. She felt herself getting dizzy, but the wind came around again and wrapped itself around her fragile mind and body, and the wind held her up. She stood straight for the occasion of living her life. She shook her head sideways, and back, and forth. She remembered her purpose. She stood vigilant for the ugly intruders.

She looked in the distance for the man that was to bring her family food. She hoped for even a glimpse of his coming in the distance. She waited and waited. The man who was the courier did not come. Her feet were tired from standing so long on the cold ground. She knew that she couldn't sit in the snow. She found the strength to tear off branches from the pine tree in front of her. As strong, and as mighty, and as indomitable the tree appeared to be, its branches bent easily, and the dead branches on the bottom, of course, were easy to cut into with a pen knife easily. She took one dead branch as a make-shift cane, and she sat down on the bed-like couch that she had made out of the pine branches. She rested her feet as she massaged her legs. She did not wish to sit for too long, however.

She hunched her shoulders up high, pushed herself up by pressing hard on one hand and then on the other hand. With the makeshift cane in one hand, she was up, standing upright, but almost rigid to her thoughts. She knew that she could die from the hovering of bleak thoughts and the rethinking of thoughts about what was going to happen. "Dying was just not her thing", she said, "Not today, not ever".

She remembered that fateful day when Joseph, and she, and the children were taken off of the train. She cried while thinking about it, but then she realized that she had to live a life without her sisters and their children and that is the way that it was. Stark thoughts presented themselves in her mind. She remembered the baby that cried and cried in the train, while its mother tried to comfort it. She remembered the little girl who was calling for her mother and was crying, because she could not find her mother. She remembered the old man that stood near the door of the train. He was planning to escape as soon as the Nazis opened the door. But she remembered that this idea was futile. She remembered. She remembered. She remembered the teenage boy who pried some of the planks open with his bare hands on the top of the car and squeezed through the space and jumped into the nearby woods and escaped. She remembered. She remembered. Then she realized that these thoughts were making her sick. She chocked up some spit. She spit the saliva on the ground. Then she opened her eyes wider. She said, "I had better start to think about good things or this war is going to kill me too.

She tried hard to think of only good things. Her wedding popped into her mind. She started to think about Joseph when he was young and when he was handsome. Joseph had come back from school in Germany. He had the benefit of a good education. He was ready to make something of himself. The only job around the area at that time was sawing down trees in the woods. Joseph had no hesitation about taking the job. He went to saw down trees in the woods. He joined the other men from the town in felling the trees, and he was well-liked and worked well with the men. Joseph became a supervisor on the lumbering party. Then he opened his own lumbering business.

She walked a little bit into the woods, but stayed close enough to the entrance of the bunker. She mostly staggered, but the stick that she had fashioned was a help for her to lean on helped to calm her down. She staggered like a beautiful young deer that had a gnawing wound on the top of one her shoulders, but knew that he must go on to find food and try to survive. She walked around the area, but in a circle, checking her bearings at times, even if there were tears in her eyes and even if she had trouble seeing clearly. The entrance to the bunker was always in her sight.

She was dazed by all that was going on, and she knew it, but she kept her balance, and remembered her bearings. She kept her belief in the spirit and in G-d and this sustained her. She asked herself the key question, "How much longer is this war going to go on?" She leaned at times very heavily on her stick. Her feet were a little swollen from sitting around too much in the bunker. She leaned on the crutch for moral support and to make sure that she did not innocently trip over a branch or slip on some ice that she did not notice.

The small branches under her feet crackled as she walked, but did not disappear into the earth. The branches were resilient. She blew her nose and felt better. To her, it was as though the earth was resistant to swallowing up any more creatures or even branches for the day. To her, the earth was protesting all of the dead that it had to swallow up. Resistance was all around her and about her, and it was not only the earth. Resistance was to hunger. Resistance to her fears, resistance to the cold and chill of the weather, and there was the resistance to the Nazis. Yes. Yes. This resistance was a type that had to be defined and remembered against every moment of the day. There was the key to the resistance against the Nazis. They were the destroyers of life, love, and hope, and people, and people's dreams. Their marching feet echoed defiance and resistance to all. Defiance was what it was all about now. Resistance was all around her. Resistance was in the partisans. Resistance was in the Americans who were landing on Europe and retaking vital cities in countries. Resistance was in the Russians who were fierce fighters and would rather die than lose the war to the Germans. Resistance would be the winner. Yes. She promised herself. She would pray to G-d for this wish to come true. This was a good feeling to her. The feel of the resistance gave her hope. She almost stopped leaning on her crutch. She stood standing by the side of the pine trees as though she was one of the trees, and she realized that this was so, and when the thought occurred to her, she laughed out loud.

The animals of the forest were resisting. They were resisting the cold and the chill. They were searching for food and finding their food. They were resisting the shattering bombs, and the dying, and burned out cores in the land. Her children were resisting. They were promising her that they wanted to live. Her children were sharing the one Bible, and the one prayer book that they had brought along with them. Joseph had carried the Bible and the prayer book all wrapped up in a sack on his back. Her husband, Joseph, was resisting as he always did, but lately he was sleeping a lot. Anna was worried.

Somewhere, oh, somewhere out there were others who were clinging onto hope and trying their best to survive. For a moment many rushing thoughts converged into her mind, as she thought, "Maybe I could help other people. If only I could see them. I would speak with them. I would tell them that the angels have come down from Heaven to help them. I would tell them to hold on. I would tell them to hold on with every breath and fiber of their bodies. Hope will come". She staggered and leaned most of her weight on the crutch. She realized she was tired. Yet she was unsure whether she should remain outside to look for the partisan who was coming to bring them food.

Her thoughts wandered. She thought, "Somewhere, resistance fighters were coming to kill off all of the Nazis", and she paused her thinking as she shook her head back and forth. She paused and asked herself the question, "When are the Russians coming?" She paused and shook her head backwards and forwards and asked, "When are the Americans coming to liberate us?" She cried, but then she blew her nose and wiped her eyes with her handkerchief. She knew that she had to think that way. She knew that she had to be strong.

Finding the Truffles

The snow from the past three days had covered up most of the ground. Little crystals in the snow glittered from the waning rays of the sunshine that managed to filter through the air. The glitter from the crystals radiated out to the sky, creating an iridescent arc that arched throughout the sky. Her eyes followed the direction of the lines of the arc. Then she turned and as she did, she stepped heavily on a branch and just happened to look down. The snow had covered the branches that lay fallen, but some of the rays of the sun had melted the upper layers of ice. There was a thin crust of ice and snow combination on the branches, and she was so happy to see that some of the ground was showing. Her eyes spotted what looked like truffles. She yelled out, "I see truffles", and she bent down and pulled at them harder and harder with all of her might and with both hands, leaving the cane on the ground, until the truffles released their tinsel hold on their roots beneath the ground, and she muttered to herself, "Now I know where to look for truffles and probably wild mushrooms".

Even though she had not eaten for two days, she felt her strength returning. She put some of the truffles into her large pockets. She fit some of the truffles into the lining of her coat through the end of the sleeve where some of the lining had worn off. She carried some of the truffles in her hands. She knew what to do. She was going to throw down most of the truffles into the entrance of the hideout bunker and then she was going to climb down the ladder. She hurried. She knew to close the hatch of the hideout very securely once she was inside. She got to work cutting the truffles as soon as she took off her coat. She put the truffles in the little make shift stove that her husband and sons had built and the truffles sizzled in their own juices. She woke up her husband and her children and she announced with a smile on her face, "Come. We have something good to eat". Her husband and children awoke with a start. Cold sores covered the lips on her children's faces. They walked over to the make-shift kitchen table, which was a huge log that they had dragged and had been thrown down into the tunnel of their new existence. They sat on the floor and leaned over the table. It, the truffles was good and Joseph and her sons would later put legs on the table and make make-shift chairs so they could sit comfortably to eat their food. Her husband and her four sons and their daughter were revived from their glazed sense of hopelessness and daze and were revived by the food. Anna knew that she had to go outside every day to search for food from the forest. Maybe her husband could go outside with her another day. Maybe one of her sons could go outside with her on another day, but they had begun to act as though they were given up. "That was wrong. That is wronging them and they are so innocent. I must help them", she said to herself.

It snowed again that night. The family could hear the winds roar and tear into the fibers of the sleeping grasses during the night. The rocking and pacing of the winds was frightening and startling at times. As tired as they felt, they could not fall asleep. The snow fell softly outside, but small drops of the cold prisms of snowflakes came inside the bunker through the natural crevices between the wooded shingles of the makeshift roof. The winds drove the little snowdrops in and the snowdrops were welcome. They were almost like little people. Martin held some of the snowdrops in his hand. Edith did the same and watched as the snowdrops melted in her hands. The two siblings drew pictures of snowflakes in the sands of the soft earth-like floor. The exhaust hole for the stove almost tooted its own horn as the winds filtered through it. The exhaust hole was well hidden, but it was covered with branches and sometimes the branches blew away with the fierce winds. They knew that their makeshift roof would hold, though. The roof of their bunker had been made from pine boughs and glued with the pine sap and made to look like the branches had fallen to the earth in a natural way. Still, some of the snow drops fell into the bunker. Every time that the snow drops blew in, they were a welcome sight. They provided a little water for them to drink, but Anna had brought some snow for water and when it melted they had pure water to drink. On their little stove, many times while they were waiting for food to be delivered, Anna had put a pot with some of the snow, and as the water was boiling, she put in some pine needles. Anna and her husband put a large bowl under one of the pine trees and they had collected the snow. It was as she told her husband, Joseph, "manna falling from the sky".

The Next Day Was Again a Struggle for Food

This day began with the shining of the sun. The light filtered into the bunker through the small draft holes. They now had light. They now were revived by eating the truffles and now by the light. Anna was resolved to finding more food for her family. She reached the trap door of the bunker, as she finished climbing up the next to the last step on the strong rungs of the ladder. She listened for footsteps. She did not hear any. She peered out of the opening as she held the hatch tight, and she was resolved to close the hatch tightly if she saw Nazi soldiers in the area. When she felt secure in her heart that there were no Nazis nearby, she pushed a little more and the trap door began to open easily. She gave that one final push with the force of her right fist, and the door opened up. The stillness of the inside of the bunker dissipated in her mind. She opened her eyes wider to view what she knew was a picture of life above the ground.

Anna's Vision of the Forest

The still life scene above the bunker of life teeming in the forest in its full essence was breathtaking to her. The pine trees were dripping off some of the snow that had fallen on their branches. The light itself was so bright. The light was enervating and she walked into what she called her garden of contentment. There were many shades of vibrant, dark green hues on all of the life. "This must be G-d's color", she said to herself. Green, shining shades of green color was the expression of smiles on the trees, wild grasses, shrubs, and even the plant life in the lake. Even a little green grass showed as it overcame its fright over the chill of the cold ground and re enervated itself with the heat from the shining sun. This was where she had stood that cold, frosty day before this day.

The forest burst with a natural movement, a burst of the flavor from nature, and, too, a movement of music in the air. Tree branches drooped and after the snow was released, the branches propped upwards and aimed towards the sky. Snow fell from the drooping branches of the beech trees too. Birds flew from branch to branch, chirping and singing to each other. They were happy. A few of the robins pecked at the wild grasses where the snow had evaporated under the long arms of the pine trees. A deer was seen running towards the mountain in a distance. It was leaping in an even, steady grace and with a steady pace. It flowed through the air as though it was floating to a soft melody of music. Anna could hear the symphony of the music in the forest. It was soothing to her thoughts.

Cheryl Freier

The Sunshine from outside the Bunker Provides Warmth and a Feeling of Comfort in the Bunker

From a short distance below in the bunker, her sons, and her daughter, and her husband looked up towards the hatch. The fresh air that blew through the small branches revived them too. Their clothes looked worn, yet they got warmth still out of the clothes. The shining sun warmed their spirits. It was not a day for them to venture. They felt safer in their hideout. They wanted to stay near the lower rungs of the ladder, and into the constancy, and the unchanging world in their underground bunker. They could not face going out above in the wilderness for this day. They had gotten used to the routine of eating soups. Anna was quite inventive with her skills to make soup out of grasses, out of onions, and out of potatoes. They got used to playing chess with each other. They got used to reading the Bible. They got used to discussing the Bible. Martin, however, thought that he might go out later and said to his father, "I would like to go stand by mother". His father agreed, but first they waited for Anna to return with some food. She always came in with snow, and they liked seeing her carrying the compacted snow.

Anna looked out into the open. She saw the small cluster of trees, which she knew was nearby the bunker. It was comforting for her to see that the trees were still there. All of the branches were extended for now even though some of them were slightly weighted down by the snow. The sun was so bright that the snow disappeared quickly from the branches of the pine trees. She liked to see some of the branches reaching out to the sky. She almost always thought that the pine trees were reaching out to G-d. The pine trees were a bright colored green and not paling, and this pleased her. She liked the nice fresh green color shades. It gave her a feeling of hope. It helped her to believe that she would someday be free and not a slave to her fears. The trees around her appeared to be untouched by the destruction of the war. This pleased Anna so much. It gave her strength to resist the Nazis and go on with her life.

❀   ❀   ❀

Anna and the Pine Trees and the Beech Trees and the West Wind Dance In the Sky

Anna began to feel tired. Her thinking about how difficult it was for her during the war wore her out. She leaned against the tall pine tree that was in front of her. It stood tall and firmly, and she admired its strength. She closed her eyes for a moment, and perhaps it was more than a moment. The tree moved towards her. The tree extended a thick branch towards her, and reached out to her, and held her hand with finger shaped pine needles from one of its small branches. The tree talked, too, and Anna's eyes widened with astonishment, as she listened to what the tree had to say. The tree told her that he understood all about what the war was doing to people and would help her. She asked the tree, "Why would you want to help me?" The tree happily responded by saying, "Why don't you remember how you brought wood for the fireplaces for the poor Christian people"? Anna smiled and said, "Yes. I did. I even helped to deliver some of the poor women's babies". "Well", said the tree, "It is time that someone helped you".

Anna remembered and she was happy once again. It was so good to be recognized for goodness. She for a brief moment forgot about her worries over her tragic situation. The tree asked her politely, "Would you like to dance with me to the beat of the rhythm of the forest?" Anna laughed at the thought of dancing with a tree. It was the first time that she had laughed in many weeks. She answered the tree, "I will dance with you, but show me what types of steps you would like to dance". Together they danced gracefully, and they danced in circles around and around the other trees, and kicked up their legs, and waved their hands and shook their hands out in the open.

The tree was free and so was she now for these moments in time. "Free", she thought to herself. Free. Free to dance. Free to do whatever I want to do." The other trees in the forest looked at the two dancing with their feet in simultaneous step. Two trees then joined in to dance with them, and they all held hands, and they all kicked their legs. Four trees joined them and danced the same step, one, two three, four and then kick and then the same steps over and over again. Soon eight trees joined them to the beat of the thunder, and the roar of the winter winds, and the beat of the pulsating earth underneath their feet. Soon sixteen other trees joined them and they all danced in unison to the beat of the roaring and thundering winds and the beat of the pulsating earth. They danced faster and faster until they were dancing faster than the winds could blow.

The west wind watched them and called out to them, "I am faster than all of you". The west wind swooped around them and lifted them up. They all danced the same steps higher into the sky. The west wind swooped around groups of two trees and lifted each group up higher than the others. Then the west wind lowered the group of two trees. They still danced in the air, but were lower than the rest of the line of dancing trees. Then the west wind quickly swooped up another two tree dancers and lifted them up higher than the others and then lowered them and lifted them up higher and then lowered them. Two by two the west wind lifted up some of the trees and then put them down.

Then the rapture of the wind increased, and it pushed all of the trees up and then pushed all of the trees down. Up and down they all went, and up and down. Anna and the trees still danced. They danced over to the beech trees and danced in a circle around them. They danced and they danced. They got happier and happier. The birds in the forest flew over them and chirped their songs while floating in the air above them. The frogs in the small ponds jumped out of the ice that covered the ponds and danced up and down and then dived down deep into the pool. They came up and then dived down continuously to the rhythm of the beat. A deer came along and jumped up high into the sky. The deer pranced in the sky in a semi-circle, which was heading up and then heading down, as he was following a rainbow. The deer turned once and danced over the crest of the rainbow and landed on the other side and then he danced to the other side of the rainbow over and over again. Little drops of rain began to fall. The rain drops would fall and then they would rise. Then some of the rain drops would fall and some of the rain drops would rise. They did this over and over again and they reached above the dancing trees and Anna. The fish in the lake wondered what all of the excitement was all about. They jumped up and pierced holes in the ice. They would jump up through the ice and then dive deep into the water.

The trees were starting to get dizzy, and so was Anna, but the west wind did not abate its fierce force. Some of the birch trees gritted their leaves and fastened the leaves to their branches. The pine trees shook from fright. Anna started to get a headache. The east wind saw what Anna and the trees were experiencing, and she felt it was very unfair. She watched the west wind very carefully, and when the west wind stopped for a moment to catch its breath, she blew at the west wind harder and harder until the west wind had to blow in another direction. The east wind grabbed hold of Anna, and all of the pine trees, and all of the beech trees. The east wind set them all down on the ground. The beech trees immediately took root. The pine trees immediately took root. Anna stood looking dazed, but her feet were planted firmly on the ground.

Slowly, the heightened momentum of the music had slowed down. The lone tree that had begun the dancing with Anna stayed with her by her side and held Anna's hand, and he was the last to go back to his place and take root. Anna was shaken by the chill of the west winds. Anna awoke from her dream. She was a much happier person now. She said to herself, "Oh my, what a dream. What a dream". She looked for the pine trees, and they were still standing. She looked for the birds, and they were still flying from branches to branches, and they were still chirping their bird calls—talking to each other. She looked for the fish and they were nowhere to be seen for the lake was frozen solid and covered with thick ice. Anna looked for the frogs and they were nowhere to be seen for they were hiding under the ice of the waters in the lake. "Oh, my", she said to herself. I must have fallen asleep and dreamed this all up. She smiled and the sun shined upon her. She felt the comfort of the warmth of the sun. She said, "I am going to be all right". She said, "My family is going to be all right". We are going to survive this war after all. She closed her eyes. She kept her eyes shut. She thought of the siege of Jerusalem and the destruction of the second temple. Visions of the people fleeing from the dangers of the fires and the heat of the flames, which was all over the buildings, and the grounds, and the rooftops was vivid in her mind. People were running, fleeing in all directions. Panic was written on the expression of every face of every man, woman, and child. The evading soldiers on horseback were pursuing men as they ran away to save themselves. Looters ran out of the Temple in Jerusalem with precious items that could not be replaced. Anna opened her eyes for she did not wish to see these visions any more. With a clear voice and wide-open eyes, she recited the words that came to her mind in clearness and clarity, "Lonely is the city that was once great with people". She shook her head. She began her vigil once again for the man was coming to bring them some food. After a long, long time of waiting for the partisan to bring food, she felt tired and relaxed by closing her eyes.

She opened up her eyes, and the tree was standing still as she had seen the tree a few moments ago. She laughed and thought as bad as it is, "I am thinking that to have lived in the times of the siege of Jerusalem was worse". She reached her hands out to the sky and prayed for peace and an end to this dreadful war. She cried, "When G-d, when G-d, "will all of the fighting and destruction end?" And it was as though the voice of an angel was speaking to her to answer her question. Anna thought that she heard a man say, "Take heart. The war will end soon." Anna felt comforted and she became calmer.

She said, "burr", because she felt cold and the weather was getting colder". She said, "I must have been dreaming—all that has happened has happened in my dreams". She breathed in and out slowly. She laughed out loud just for a second. She felt freedom. She could feel the free-blowing wind blowing into mouth and into nostrils. She breathed in and out again and again, and she felt like the weight of all the worrying was lifted from her mind. She decided to sing a lullaby. She sang. She sang a lullaby tune that she had always sung to her children when they had difficulty going to sleep. She said, "Yes. I must have been dreaming". Then she thought, "Do you think that it would be possible to dance in the sky with trees?" She shrugged her shoulders.

❀   ❀   ❀

Plans Are Being Made In Town To Bring the People In the Woods Foods

Under the cover of darkness, Joseph's foreman knocked on the doors of a few house in the town. He was told to come into the houses immediately. He told each person that he or she should knock on the doors of houses of people that they trusted and that they knew were not Nazi sympathizers. They were to meet in the church on the top of the hill in the town shortly after it became dark. One by one the men left their houses and went into the church.

❋   ❋   ❋

Anna Searches for Her Contact

She looked today again for their contact. She stood by the side of the tall pine tree and looked in all directions for the man who was to bring the family the food. She asked herself, "How will he find us? There is so much new snow that has fallen over the last few days, and it is very cold out", but then she reminded herself that he had always found them before. She shook her head in marvel, as she thought the war has brought out the best and the worst that is within us people. The foreman's assistant was the last person on earth that she would ever consider as a person good enough to risk his own life in order to save her family. He was a little younger than most of the other farmers. He married young and had two small children to care for. He hardly spoke to people. He was quieter than most people. He took care of a wife and two daughters. There was always food on their table. He always came home for dinner. He was up bright and early to begin a new day looking for opportunities to make a living, but always farming.

Anna thought to herself, "As bad as it is now, it would have been a lot worse, if we had stayed on the train. And she said to herself, "Getting off of that train was a miracle in itself." She cried and she said, "I still cannot believe that we managed to get off of that train". She cried, "We never looked back". Her mind pulsated back and forth for a moment, and paced, and she thought of the story of Lot and his wife Sarah and their two daughters who had escaped the wrath of G-d when he destroyed the two cities, Sodom and Gemorrah. Lot was told not to look back and so was his wife, but she disobeyed the command and as a result of her looking back, she turned into a pillar of salt. This was recorded in history. This was recorded in the Bible.

Anna said, "That is recorded in history for all to read about and all to discuss". She said as she remembered what her husband always tried to tell her, "This too will pass. This too will pass and everything will be all right. The truth wins out. All the innocent victims who died in this war will be vindicated. God will make them into angels and they will do G-d's work of mercy and goodness throughout the world" She said, "Amen to that". She remembered a portion of one of the major parts of the prayer service for during the day, the Amidah. She repeated the words that she remembered and she felt as though the west wind and the east wind was carrying her words of prayers to others who needed the comfort of these same words.

She heard the hatch to the bunker open, and she turned around, quickly with an almost instinct to fight, and she saw her son, Martin. She had come out of the bunker. It seemed to her for just that moment that he had gotten taller. Even though she had seen him about an hour ago, she looked at him with a sense of freshness, a sense of welcoming that would make one think that she had not seen him for a while. She adored her son more for coming outside to be with her. She blessed G-d that she was here and that she was able to hold her son's hand. She reminded herself how precious life is.

Her son, who was one of her four sons stood next to her. She ran her hand through his hair gently, and he immediately pushed away and said, "Ma", "I am all grown up. He was asserting himself as a man. "This was one good thing that came out of this war," Anna said to herself. "My sons are all grown up". She paused and thought, "They understand the realities of this war". She held his hand. His hand was cold. She said to him, "I can go inside with you. I think that you are too cold to be outside", but he insisted on being there by her side, while she looked for the man who was coming to bring the family food. He joined her in her search.

The Plaguing Sounds of the Battle Had Erupted

The resistance and the war had been coming a long time to Slovakia. It was surprising that an uprising did not erupt sooner than what history records. The army of the Slovaks was airlifted to France and to England when the Nazis took over Czechoslovakia. At first the deposed government fled to France. Soon the exiled President of Czechoslovakia realized that his government in exile would have to flee France, because the Nazis were invading France and taking over the country. Benes and his government and many of the troops from Slovakia fled to England and were welcome in England. Slovakian air men flew missions over Germany and risked their lives the same way the British pilots risked their lives.

When Hitler invaded Russia, the Russians made the decision to recognize the Czechoslovakian leadership in exile. Since December of 1943, there was a treaty between the exiled government that Benes was in charge of and which was located in England and the Soviet government. It was designed to be a treaty of friendship, but it was really designed to join powers that could become cohesive and knock out the Germans in every world sphere that the Germans had dominated. The Slovaks who were considered part of Czechoslovakia did not wage war against the Germans until the day after the puppet head of Slovakia, Josef Tiso announced that it was his wish to recognize that the Germans were the rulers of Slovakia. Tiso made this announcement on August 28, 1944. One day afterwards in a direct answer to Tiso, the Slovaks went to war to win back their country. Actually, the Slovaks had been waiting for an excuse to fight to regain their country. Up until this August date, the Germans did not fight against the Slovakian Partisans on Slovak soil. The Germans were fighting now on Slovak soil, and they were killing soldiers and innocent civilians mercilessly. The Germans had no remorse. The Nazi soldiers were robotic in nature. They were trained to kill. They killed whoever was in their sights.

❊   ❊   ❊

Fighting Had Gotten Worse in Slovakia

Now it was a new situation for all of the people who lived in Slovakia. It was a worse terrifying experience for the Jews who had managed to survive the war thus far. The insurgent's uprising lasted for 61 days and everyone knew instantly when the fighting had stopped. All guns had stopped, the shouting had stopped. The dying had stopped. The chance of freedom now was all but doomed for the Germans had squashed the Slovakian insurgents. Now that there was occasional fighting in the street in towns in Slovakia, the only hope that the family had was to remain in the woods.

They escaped to the woods in August of 1944 as soon as the fighting between the insurgents and the Germans had started. Now it was winter. Now it was December of 1944. Now it was a bitter cold winter and there were still two or more months of winter to survive through. Without the help of Joseph's foreman, they found safety and built a bunker in the woods. The family was brought food, and clothing by trusted men that Joseph's foreman believed in. Otherwise, they would have frozen to death or starved to death. Now it was the winter of 1944 and the Freier family was isolated and alone in a far off hiding spot, which was deep in the woods and was near the mountains in Slovakia.

Anna wondered if she and her family would survive. It was a day-to-day struggle to keep from remembering the fear of being hunted. It was a day-to-day struggle to release the memories of dear ones whom the Nazis had taken and put on transportation trains. Her thoughts wandered to think about her eldest niece, Elsa.

Joseph, her husband, had contacted other leaders in the Micholovce community. They made a plan to smuggle out the brightest and the young persons with the most promise for a good life. Where would they go? They would be sent to families in Hungary, gentile people whom they knew could be trusted. Some of the leaders in the community and Joseph had known Hungarian gentile families for years and had done business with these families for years. Elsa, Anna's eldest niece was told that she would have a chance to leave Micholovce, because of the growing environment and Joseph and many others knew that it was just a matter of time before the Nazis would take over the town and patrol the streets. It would be much harder to escape from the Nazis then. It was a hope amongst the leaders in Micholovce that the war would never come to Hungary and that Elsa and some of the other youth that were chosen would escape unscathed from the hunger, and deprivation, and the monstrous killing in the war. Elsa was a budding student. She was in the middle of her last year in college. She was told to leave the country. She was told everything about her escape from Micholovce and she left. She was given false papers, which had all of the realism of authenticity. She rode on the train to Hungary, knowing that she would probably never see any of her relatives again. She embarked on the train all alone. She carried a small satchel. There was no ceremony. She said her goodbyes in secret and at home.

❊　❊　❊

Information On The Nazi Foes

The Nazis were a bitter group of men who were not necessarily from humble upbringing. Some of the Nazi leaders had grown up very wealthy. Some had been brought up in one of the many castles that existed in Germany in that time and day. Each and every one of the leaders had an infinite appetite for power and they were hungry for money, and the riches, and the status that comes with power. In seeking more and more power, they meant to rule all of Europe and Russia, and they had thoughts about taking over the United States, too. They had definite plans and meant to conquer all of the countries in the world. The leaders of the Nazis had an insatiable appetite for power and conquering. They planned for aggrandizement with the mindset for ruling the world. They had a vision of the type of world that they would want to live in. They were, all of the leaders desirous to be rulers of castles and large estates. It was not enough for them to own large, massive lands and valuable properties. They wanted to create a lasting Paradise for themselves, a new world of dominance for themselves.

❀   ❀   ❀

The Nazis were Very Versed in History

The Nazis were very versed in their history especially since they were defeated in WWI. The history of the Germans being warmongers and being pugilistic and being badly defeated goes back to the Thirty Years War, which took place between the years 1618 to 1648. The medieval ruler most known to have ruled over the German people was Charlemagne. The capital city for the ruler, Charlemagne was Aachen City. This particular city, Aachen City is now part of the present vast territories of Germany.

The German people were badly defeated in this war, the Thirty Years War. Their fields and much of their lands lay plundered and untilled for many years. It is significant to note, too, that before the year 1871, the German people were a group of tribes, reputed to be part of the Frank's empire. The empire of the Franks, incidentally, included not only the German tribes, it included the Dutch people, the Flemish people, and the French people. Until the declaration of the German state in 1871, which meant the establishment of Germany as an entity by itself, a virtual country by itself, the government of Germany did not exist. Until this formation of Germany as a national state in its entirety, the country of Austria was considered to be owned by the German territories even though the Austrian people were not of a German heritage.

They, the Nazis had in mind and formulated plans to create a Garden of Eden in which they were the Lords and rulers of all of the people. They wanted to recreate a time in medieval history. The Nazis wanted to be the rulers of lands, and rulers of castles, and wanted the power of the decision of life or death over its citizens. The Nazis were so emotionally ill at this particular time in history that they fantasized this whole creation of a new world where they were the masters, and the kings, and the people were their serfs, and the servants. This plan for the Garden of Eden seemed to fit in with plans for a feudal, vassal country of Germany. The Garden of Eden was their choice castle as they knew that this was the haven in heaven and they wanted it. This was their land that they designated to be Holy. This was their land in which slowly they would re introduce to the people in the world the animals from long, long ago who were long extinct. This was a major part of the Nazi plan. It was a psychological delusion that was fantasy, but definitely indicative of their brutal emotional mentality. This is the plan that Hitler implemented with his leaders and followed, and it was supposed to be the best plan for the Germany people. In reality, it was a plan to make him king over all of the people in the world.

Hitler Had Plans to Be The Ruler of A Vast Empire

It was a plan for Hitler to be the ruler of a vast empire. He would live in a magnificent castle, which was built so high that from the distance it looked like the castle was entering the sky. He would have his own black stallions and white stallions and would be accompanied by a group of 100 gallant knights, holding up the banner and the crest of the German people and naming Hitler king. Hitler would ride on his magnificent stallion, and all of the surfs, and workers would bow down their heads as he passed them by. He would never acknowledge any of these people. After all, they were just workers and to Hitler they were not important enough, and for to Hitler, these people were beneath his social status. Hitler would ride throughout the countryside and view all of his lands. He would watch as the crops grew and the workers sold their crops. He would then ride with all of his men throughout the countryside and exact high taxes on all of these working people. Hitler would return home, and there would be merriment and frolicking in the all the halls of the castle. There would be wines from all of the many vineyards. There would be roasted pigs on a spit for all to pull apart and enjoy eating. Dogs in the kitchen would bark for the choicest pieces of meats and the meats would be given to them. Cats would scrounge around the table after the merriment and eat the meats from the plates that were left on the tables. All would be merry, merry, and merriment, but only for Hitler and his band of evil cutthroats.

To this end and purpose of self-fulfillment and of a dynasty, Hitler participated in the genetic alteration and experimentation on groups of people. Physical deformities of one sort or another was the lot of those poor souls who were his victims for this experimentation. The Nazis experimented in creating the ultimate bomb, but thankfully and fortunately, these plans never came to fruition. The Nazis wanted to alter the natural order of G-d's creation of animals. They wanted to redefine death, and dying, and bring back life into those animals that were known to be extinct.

To this purpose and end, one of their initial experiments was ordered by Hitler himself. Hitler wanted the recreation genetically of a cow that had become extinct during the 1600's. This was a very large cow. It was not the typical domestic, placid cow that grazes on the grases of pastures all day. It was a highly aggressive cow, and it was known for attacking other cows and other animals. indeed, Hitler did give an assignment to two biologists, the Heck brothers to recreate the extinct ancient wild bull and, the auroch. The auroch was known to be extinct in the 1600's. The heck brothers did genetically create a bull that was very similar in appearance to the auroch by cross-breeding many breeds of bulls and cows. The recreated auroch had a behavior that was extremely aggressive. It would fight with other animals constantly. It had a sense of kill that was woven into the fibers, within its genetic makeup. It was in no way docile like other cows. In a sense, the re creation of this cow was exactly the type of animal that they wished to create for the world to see. The re creation was a mirror image of their own thoughts of aggression and viciousness. Aggression was the Nazis way of life. They could not live any other way. Their illusion of fantasy protected them in this aggressive mode of thought. The recreation fit in very well with the Nazis life style, and for a while they got away with all of their aggressions and killings of people indiscriminately, and they were adamant about designing plans for the removal of anyone who stood in their way.

❀ ❀ ❀

Hitler Planned to Bring to the World a Recreation of an Extinct Cow

Hitler's German soldiers and a team were ordered to bring back this cow that had become extinct for well over hundreds of years. They believed so much in their own powers and they felt that they had a capability that went well beyond any sense of normal norm and purpose. They believed that they had the power to create and alter genetically their own choices of both animals and people. They believed then that they had been touched by G-d to change the order of life and living in the world. In reality, however, this madness and sociopathic behavior was in the very defiance of G-d himself. In reality, this behavior was in defiance of all that civilizations had managed to build and to create for the benefit of man and for the benefit of all living creatures up to this period in history.

The behavior of the Nazis was so bad and evil that it was in the very defiance of G-d himself, and in defiance of all men of reason, and integrity, and men who read the Bible and believed in worshipping G-d. The behavior of the Nazis was complete lawlessness. The behavior of the Nazis was wanton and this behavior had to be destroyed by leaders of many countries and as soon as possible. Fortunately, with the intervention and coming ashore of thousands and thousands of American soldiers, the British now had a fighting chance to overthrow the vicious Nazi armies and liberate the innocent people and soldiers in France and Italy, and in other countries where the Nazis maintained a stronghold.

The German Nazis Would Meet Their Fate after the Invasion of Normandy

It was the ringing of a bell for doom, and a death knell, and fateful day in Normandy for the Nazi usurpers and killers that had launched their rockets of hatred, when early in the morning, the American 101st United States Airborne Division landed on the shores of Europe. The armies of men trained to fight and defeat the monster dragons of hatred and spit-fires, these bravest of the brave American soldiers sailed in small boats, sailing on the rough waters onto the beach behind Utah Beach. It was a surprise attack and the Germans although fortified, and killing, and maiming, and wounding many, many American soldiers were ultimately driven from the beach. This was the beginning of the end of the forceful hatred and hallucinations of self-grandeur that the Nazis imbued themselves with. Word of the conflict spread rapidly from household to household and every woman, man, and child hailed and praised the American for coming to their rescue. Hitler could not keep this information of Nazi defeat a secret as he had done for so long with the killing and maiming of innocent people and Jewish people and Gypsy people. The American, and the British, and the Russians were able to win battles and re conquer all city after city that the Nazis had managed to conquer.

❉ ❉ ❉

Anna and Her Family Could Hear the Sounds of the Battles

The sound of battle erupted. Fire, and cannon balls, and bombs, and aimed bullets flew through the air in scattered directions, as they hissed and whizzed to their targets in the distant and nearby towns, and in Anna's town, Micholovce. The sounds of guns being cocked and the snap of the trigger on riffles reverberated from one mountain peak to the other, giving all who heard the startling sounds the shuddering feeling, a sense of agonizing fear of where the next bullet would be aimed at. Intermittently the gunfire of the cannons was released with a booming sound that was a resounding sound. It echoed and echoed past all time and back into space. There were other sounds, too, that could be heard. The sounds of the screaming of the wounded could be heard for miles

44

and miles. The sounds of soldiers shouting commands to each other could be heard from a long distance away. The echoes of time carried the voices for all to hear. The sounds of buildings exploding from the exploding bombs could be heard from mountain top to mountain top. The pristine lands of the forest had protected innocent people who were prey to the Nazis and helped them to find refuge, but no one could find refuge from the startling and distinguishable sounds, and its piercing targets. Shrapnel filled the air as though it was a swarm of locusts flying to consume the corn crops. The winds blew the sounds into the air from town to town. The winds blew the dust from the exploding and imploding buildings all over the sky and into the pure forms of the pristine lake waters in the forest. The waters carried the blood from the dead and the wounded for miles downstream. The ground shook and groaned from the fallen that would sink into the abyss and forgetfulness. Many, many lives cut short, and rich talents, and treasures of the mind forgotten forever. Dreams shattered in moments. There was still hope in Anna Freier's mind for survival. She prayed a lot. She was adamant in not giving up hope.

❀　❀　❀

Anna Dreams about Riding on a Cloud and Floating Away in the Air

Anna was tired. She was worn from listening to the sounds of gun fire and battle. She was fatigued from wondering if the war and the fighting would move into the woods. A cloud hovered above her. It was a rather large cloud, with fringes of circles all around its circumference. Anna extended her hands to the cloud and reached out of the cloud. They pulled her up, and she disappeared into the sky. She floated on the cloud as though the cloud was a magic carpet. She breathed in the fresh air. The air did not have the smell of the residues of war. It was filtered from the residues that were polluted. She could see the bunker beneath her, and she called out to her children and to her husband, but they did not hear her voice. They were not interested in going outside this day. She said to herself, "Somehow I must find the strength to continue. I must go up the ladder and go outside every day. That way my family will know that they have to do right by themselves. They have to go on living and that means going outside. She hesitated, "They all seemed happier staying down in the bunker". She shook her head in dismay and as she did, the cloud rocked from side to side. She held onto the sides of the cloud for dear life at first. Then she realized that the cloud was trying to help her to understand more about what was happening in the woods and also what was happening in their town of Micholovce. She looked intently and saw the outline of one female angel. She was guiding the cloud that she was riding on. Together she and the angels glided on the waves of the sky. They floated carefully as they were a bit fearful of the turbulence. The angels were careful to sight birds flying high in the sky, and they steered the cloud away from the birds, and easily circumvented them. The angels were fearful of battle cannon balls that flew wild through the air. They seemed to know when the cannon balls were near, and they moved out of the way of the cannon balls' trajectory. The angels were aware of airplanes intruding on the clean, clear air of the sky. The angels knew how to avoid the intruding airplanes, and they avoided them. The angles found a clear line of travel after a while in the sky. They moved to a higher shelf in the sky that was much safer. Onwards they steered the clearly white-colored cloud, which Anna found to be very plush to sit on while her legs dangled freely in the air of the sky. The angels steered towards Micholovce and it did not take them long before the cloud was sitting in the sky on the top of the town. Ana could see her street at first glance. Then she could see the row of houses on her street. Then she could see her house. "Oh", she cried voluminous tears instantly as she realized that her house was still standing. She felt for an instant that maybe she could climb off of the cloud and enter her house. She knew though that it was not possible. The Germans were fighting against the Partisans in the streets nearby to her house. It was dangerous to think such a thought even if she had the safety of the angels. The angels drove the cloud higher and continued to circle the town of Micholovce.

Cheryl Freier

Anna revisits of times that were festive in December

Anna's mind wandered as she got a little bit dizzy and her mind wandered to thoughts that she was living in that house and preparing for the Chanukah celebration. She had grated a whole bag full of large potatoes. Edith had helped her to peel and to grate the potatoes. Sam had helped her to grate the onions. Martin had helped her to put into the batter the four eggs and he helped her stir the mixture in the mixing bowl. She remembered how he stirred and stirred the batter with his right hand and when his right hand was tired, he mixed with his left hand. When his left hand got tired, he said, "Ma. That is enough". She smiled, and said, "'Yes, thanks very much. That is fine". She lit one of the burners on the stove with a large match, and she put some fat into the frying pan, and watched as the fat sizzled in the pan. She lifted the pan slightly from the top of the burner, and she wiggled the fat in the frying pan so that it covered the bottom of the frying pan evenly. She placed the frying pan back on the burner and lowered the control for heat on the knob. She went for the large bowl of batter. She placed a large spoon in the batter, and began to dip enough batter into the spoon, and when the spoon was filled up, she dipped the spoonfuls of the yellow-like colored potato batter into the sizzling fat. The batter instantly sizzled and the side of the batter that was burning turned quickly into a dark brown color, and then she turned over the six pancakes that fit into the frying pan and when the potato pancakes were browned on both sides, she lifted them out of the

48

frying pan and put them onto a large clean plate that she had covered with a paper napkin. She dipped some more batter into the hot oil and she made some more potato pancakes. When all of the batter was gone, and she had made over 30 large size potato pancakes, she started to cut the salad. She cut out the core of the lettuce and tore the leaves apart. She added slices of ripe, red tomatoes, and she cut some thin slices of onions, and green peppers. She tossed the vegetables around by using two large spoons in a swirling motion, and then added a drop or two of table vinegar, and she added two full tablespoons of liquid oil. She wrapped the top of salad bowl with a clean cloth and put the bowl into the refrigerator. She smelled the sumptuous aroma of chicken baking in the oven. She reached for the pot holding the large chicken with a towel covering each hand. She looked at the chicken and saw that it was brown on all sides so she knew that the chicken was done, and she shut the oven door to keep the chicken in the heat. She cut up slivers of carrots and placed them in a plate. She was ready to serve the meal. She was ready to celebrate the Chanukah holiday with her family.

She heard the footsteps running quickly down the long, circular stairwell. She heard the thud of the footsteps at the bottom of the last step. She heard running towards the kitchen. They ran through the large study, and into the enormous living room, and stopped short at the entrance of the kitchen. They each reached for a kippoh hat and placed it on their heads. They each said a silent prayer to thank G-d for the food that they were blessed to eat. Anna told Edith to light the candles, and she did, and she said a prayer over the candles. Anna coaxed Edith, "Sing the special prayer for the holiday, and she did. Anna then motioned to Martin, "Come on over and sing us a Chanukah song", and he did. His voice resonated echoes within the walls of the house, and his voice resonated resounding echoes throughout the neighborhood. Everyone listened, and felt soothed by the singing, and the songs.

Joseph came into the house to join them. He walked into the kitchen after he had taken off his hat, and coat, and hung them into the closet. He put on his kippoh, sat down, and said a blessing. He said to them all, "I am sorry that I am late". All of the children looked up and said, "Hi Pop", and Joseph smiled and nodded to them. Anna sat down and said her blessings and smiled at Joseph. Joseph nodded his head. They all reached for some food. Anna took hold of the plate with potato pancakes and she took two and placed them on her plate. She passed the plate to Josep, and he took the fork and placed the fork into three of the potato pancakes. He said quietly, "These look like the best potato pancakes that I have ever had". Anna reached for the plate with the cooked applesauce that had sprinkles of cinnamon placed on the top of the apples. Sam shoveled in the latkes and applesauce into his mouth, and then reached for the salad. Edith reached for the bread and put apple jelly on the top of the bread. All was silent as they ate the food. Joseph spoke, "I want to be truthful with you children. Things do not look good for a lot of people. Most of us Jews are in danger". Sam asked, "What type of danger? He looked at his father." Joseph gulped down some of the potato latkes and said, "We are in mortal danger. No too many people think the way I think, but I am telling you from what I see, there will be killings of Jews". Sam bent his head. Bernard's eyes widened, and he said, "Pop, can we escape"? "Well, my brother and his wife have asked for the money from their share of the business, and I am going to give it to them". He paused and then continued, "It will take a while, but I will do my best to get the money together to get us out of here". Martin asked, "Pop. Where will we go?" Joseph hesitated as though he was in deep thought, but recovered his first thought and answered, "We will head for Switzerland like a lot of other people I know are doing". Martin looked surprised, and asked, "Why Switzerland Pop?" Joseph answered as he was completely assured of the answer, and said, "Switzerland has been declared as neutral territory, and we will be safest in Switzerland. Martin nodded. Anna coaxed everyone, "Continue to eat your food, everyone". Anna's father entered from his room on the side of the kitchen, and as he sat down, he said, "Anna, I will pray that you and Joseph and the children all are safe". Anna gave him a plate of the latkes and applesauce and cut off a piece of the chicken for him. She said to her father, "Eat and enjoy", and her father, David, nodded his head in approval. Anna felt that it was better not to talk about the difficult political scene. Joseph wanted everyone to know about the dangerous political scene, and he was right.

The cloud moved. There was a bump in the ride every once in a while, but Anna knew that she would never fall off. The cloud moved to the West of the town. The cloud wiggled and jiggled as though it was a magic carpet. When the angels arrived where they wanted to go, they stopped steering the cloud. The cloud stopped right on the top of the church in town. It was a holiday. It was obvious to see for there were bright lights all over the buildings despite the war that was taking away their freedoms and taking away so much from their way of life. All of the windows were covered with small lights on the outside of the building. The pine trees were adorned with small lights that were wrapped around the tree and provided full glares of lights that brightened up everyone's hearts and souls. People were sitting in the church. A Priest was delivering a speech. There were prayers that everyone was saying and every once in a while the congregation would sing songs. Everything was very festive despite the fact that a war was raging. These few hours of prayer gave sustenance, and good cheer, and hope for the end of the war to a lot of people. Anna could see herself, and her husband, and her daughter, and her four sons sitting on one of the many benches of the church. The Priests she remembered had helped to get her family Christian papers so the Germans left Anna and her family alone. She remembered that she and her family read prayer books, and they sang the songs with everyone else.

"Yes Anna said to herself we were allowed to be Catholics and survived for at least two years as Catholics". Anna remembered some of the hymns, and she sang them. The angels steering the cloud must have heard the songs of the people's voices singing for Anna also heard the sounds of voices humming the Christmas songs. Anna and the angels could see the giant doors of the church opening. People walked out and most looked up at the sky. It was a clear night and there were only a few stars noticeable in the sky. The snow had fallen, and had been shoveled, and there were clear pathways for people to walk home on. Most of the people came in wagons that were drawn by one horse or two horses. After a while all of the people had left. The Priest stepped out of the doors to look up at the sky. He paused for a moment as though reciting a pray and then he turned and went back into the church. The lights from the inside of the church slowly receding as the doors slowly closed. All that could be seen was the lighting on the outside of the building. As the cloud steered away, the lighting got dimmer and dimmer, but Anna remembered the melodies of the songs, and it was nice to see people going to church to pray.

The cloud steered and Anna's cloud stopped at an old farm house that had been abandoned. There was a glimmer of a lighted candle in the inside of a window. Anna could see a young couple sitting on the floor and staring out to space. Anna wondered, "Would this be the way that it ends for this lovely young couple?" She summoned one of the angels and even though she could only see the outline of the angel, she knew that the angel was there?" Anna asked, "Is there something that you can do for this young couple? I see that they have lighted a candle? That means to me that they still care about living". The angel asked, "Are you afraid that the young couple is going to die?" Anna's head and shoulders shook for a few moments. She answered in a quiet voice to the angel's questions, "Yes. I am afraid that they are going to give up." "Very well then," replied the angel, and she steered the cloud to the window of the house. The angel stopped the cloud. She went into the house and tapped the two young people

53

on their shoulders. They awoke but were startled when they saw the outline of the angel. She did not want the young couple to panic, so she revealed herself as a real angel, and seeing her as a real angel made them think that they could believe in G-d. They stood up, holding each other's hands and said to the angel, "can we come along with you?" The angel replied without hesitation, "Yes. You certainly may come with me. I already have another passenger and her name is Anna". The other two angels helped the angel and the young couple to come aboard. Anna greeted the young couple and told them that the angels were helping her and that they would help them. Anna said to them without hesitation, "the angels will find you a safe place to live". She encouraged the young couple. She said, "You will survive the war and you will be all right, the both of you". The young couple held each other's hands and smiled. They could hardly mutter the words, but said, "Thank you". Anna noticed that the young couple was very hungry and that they were very cold. She summoned the angel and the angel quickly called into the clear air up in the sky for two hot bowls of lentil soup. A few minutes passed and the angel gave the young couple the bowls of soup. The angel could see that the young couple was very undernourished so she called to the air that surrounded the cloud, "Bring me some hot chocolate, and some loaves of bread, and fresh butter and strawberry preserves". She placed the food on the cloud in the front of the young couple. The young couple looked at the angels with expressions of joy and said, "thank you". The angel saw that the young couple was still very cold so she called to the air outside of the cloud and in the sky, saying "bring me some warm blankets", and in a moment two very large woolen blankets were dropped near to the young couple where they sat and enjoyed eating their soup with the breads. Anna spoke with the young couple. She explained that she and her family were living in an under the ground bunker. She explained that they were pretty safe from the Germans, but that one never knows for certain if one can elude the Germans.

❄   ❄   ❄

Anna Travels with the Angels and Meets People Who Are Resisting the Nazis

The angels steered the cloud straight and into a westerly direction. Anna at first was a little afraid about going in the Westerly direction towards Bratislava, but she knew in her heart if the angels were driving the cloud that she would be all right. They flew over the mountains and at one time, Anna thought that she saw Bernard walking around the outside of the bunker. The image of the boy was not clear, but she knew that it could be him. She said to the angels, "Maybe you should let me down. I think that I see my son looking for me". The angels replied to her, "You will meet your son soon on the same pathway. We thought that we should show you and the young couple what is happening near Bratislava". Anna hesitated, but she believed in the truth and the sincerity of the angels. She said, "Yes", in a hesitating sounding voice, and the angels nodded their approval.

The young couple looked more alert. They were sitting up and watching the view from the cover of the cloud. One of the angels spotted an airplane far, far in the distance and she could hear the motor of the airplane. She said to the other two angels. I think that this is a German airplane. Immediately one of the other two angels suggested that she change the shape of the cloud. The angel asked, "What shape should we be?" The other angel answered, "make yourself into a round, puffy ball, but leave little spaces for yourself to see and hear outside of the cloud and leave some spaces in the cloud for us to see out of it". "Will do", the lady angel answered to the male angel. Immediately a canopy of white cotton material covered them all up, but there were two small windows on each side of the outside of the puffy cloud. Anna looked through one window. The couple each looked through a window. They saw the German airplane coming. The plane did not see them. The angel who was driving dived down deep into a crescent of other clouds. A light blue, pinkish colored line suddenly appeared. The German plane flew above the blue, pinkish line and the cloud flew several feet below the blue, pinkish colored cloud. Anna and the young couple looked up to watch the German airplane as it flew by. Its motor was ticking loud and they were all that close to the plane that they could see the plane glide by in the clouds.

The angel who was driving the cloud looked at the other two angels and they looked at her. She said, "I am relieved now". One of the two men angels told her, "Perhaps we should land the cloud for a while. It may be safer for us to ride in the nighttime". The female angel replied. "Yes. I just have to find a safe place." They all looked at the terrain and one of the male angels said, "Look, there is a field of corn a mile to the right of us". She looked and saw it, and asked, "Should I land in the middle or the field, and the male angel answered, "I think that that would be your best bet. She put the cloud into gear, and they descended straight down but very slowly. The angel who was at the controls knew that it was best to go down slowly. The angel who was piloting the cloud knew to press the buttons for the landing controls and out came four feet that got longer and longer until they reached 20 feet, and then the cloud landed on the feet. The angel who was piloting the cloud pressed another button after the cloud landed and then the feet receded and the cloud was on the ground. A door to the front opened up. Two doors on the sides of the cloud opened up. The young couple got out of the cloud. Anna stayed in the cloud with the two men angels, and they watched from one of the windows in cloud.

The female angel led them into the woods. The young couple at first were fearful and stopped, but the female angel coaxed them on and extended her hand. The woman of the young couple told the young man that it would be all right. She said, "She is trying to lead us to some people where we can at least be safer than we were". The young man said, "Okay" meekly, but he knew that they were dying where they were hiding in the house. They would have died of hunger or would have died from the cold. Together they held hands and they followed the angel. The angel led them deeper and deeper into the woods. Finally, the angel stopped and said to them, "We will be walking through a clearing and most likely one or two guards will stop us". She cautioned, "Do not be afraid. I will tell you what to say," and they began to walk through the clearing in the woods. They had gone about fifty yards and were about to continue, when one man dressed in a light brown leather jacket, jumped down from one tree. Another man, taller than the first man, but clean shaven jumped down from a tree to the left, and they both aimed their rifles at the young couple. They spoke in a soft-sounding manner, but what they said had a lot of meaning. They said in a straight-forward no uncertain terms tone of voice, "raise your hands and stand still". The angel told them to do just that, but reminded them that they would be all right. The angel explained that these men were partisans. Many of them were Jewish and that they would be cared for by these partisans". She promised the young couple that she would stay with them for another few minutes. They understood her and nodded to her, but they raised their hands and they stopped right in the spot where they were. "Who are you asked the clean shaven man?" His name was Michael. Michael looked with a serious stern expression on his face, and he stood his ground, and he held the rifle pointed towards the man. The man told them that they were hiding from the Nazis. Michael listened and asked, "From what town did you come from?" The young man whose name was Jon answered, "We come from Micholovce". The young man looked at Michael with fear in his eyes, but stood still and his hands were still raised above his head. "Okay". Michael said, "One of us will walk in the front of you and one of us will walk in the back of you". The young couple looked at each other, shuddered, but they knew that they had no alternative. They walked on, but they knew that they could take one foot forward and then move the other foot forward. The young man muttered to the young lady, "We are together and that is what counts most". The young woman heard his words of encouragement and moved her head to face him and she smiled. It was a long walk. It was a long trail. The young couple could see that they would come across several other cross checks, but they remained in the trees, but their rifles were cocked. The young couple realized that they passed two more check points and the young man was counting just as a precaution. He said to himself, "We must have passed five checkpoints and they were about to enter a mountain pass. In reality, it was the mouth of a large cave and before they entered, the guard Michael raised his hand and said in a soft tone of voice, "We need to stop". Immediately out of what seemed like nowhere, five men appeared. They walked with lightning speed. One came over from a ridge on the top of the mountain. Two came from the left side of the entrance of the cave. Two of the men had been hiding behind bushes that were on the right side of the cave. All five men stood tall and erect and pointed their guns at the young couple. Michael spoke on the young couple's behalf. He told the five determined young partisan soldiers, who were determined to defend their territory that he found these two young people wandering in the woods. They said that they had come from Micholovce and that they had to escape into the wood, because the Nazis were coming again for a roundup of Jewish people. The young man interjected by saying that he and his young wife had been hiding in a cabin on an abandoned farm. He told them, "They were literally dying from starvation and from the cold in the cabin, when he heard a voice whisper into his ears saying that he should escape into the woods with his wife". He said that he followed the suggestion. He wife was glad to escape into the woods and came with him". Michael gave the five men a command, "I will be in charge of these two people. I will help them to get settled and to join our village". The five men nodded, and they raced back to their positions. Michael said to the young couple and to the soldier, who was walking behind him, "Come follow me". They walked into the cave. It was pitch black at first, but as they walked deeper and deeper into the cave, they could see openings at the top of the cave through which light was filtering through, because the partisans had chiseled chunks of rock out of the cave's exterior and out of parts of the mountain. As they got into deeper and deeper into the cave, the more the light from the hewn crevices filtered in. They walked and walked and as they walked the young couple realized that they were descending into the cave. Springs of water flowed down from the longtime crevices that had let the water flow gently down the walls of the cave, and flowed in a naturally made gutter out to the opening, and to the mouth of a lake that was located in the middle of the mountains. Michael called to the young couple, "place your hands in a cuplike way and let the pristine clear waters flow into your hands and drink from the waters. Michael cupped his hands and slurped up some of the waters, and shook his head, and went for more water. The young couple were very thirsty. They slurped up the water that was placed in their hands, and they slurped up the water very quickly. They went back for more and more. Michael called to them, "Come you will have water and wine with the group. You will dine with the group too. The young couple followed Michael. He led them to the back side entrance of the cave. There the sun shined brightly into their eyes, and they both looked up and down ridges of colors before their eyes. The backs of their eyes began to accept the light from the outside and slowly with the conglomeration of all of the colors to be seen at one time led to a vision to see an image of a rainbow. The colors of the rainbow were so very bright and vivid. The orange color blended beautifully with the yellow color that was placed beneath it. One of the top colors of the rainbow was the blue color and it radiated its blue color at the very top of the rainbow. When the young couple looked at the color blue, they felt that the color dripped into the shades of the blue shades of color of the waters of the lake. Michael called to the young couple, "Come on over. Follow me", and the young couple walked faster and followed Michael to the edge of the waters of the lake. The other soldier walked briskly and came over to the lake. Michael waded into the waters of the edge of the lake. The young couple followed. The young lady lifted up her skirt so that she could avoid getting the edges wet. The other soldier met up with Michael and they climbed into a row boat. Michael took the oars and he called to the young couple, "Come on over. Come into the rowboat". The young woman entered the rowboat first, sitting down on the ledge on the back of the boat and her husband sat right next to her. The waters appeared to be muddy and starting off into the waters with the rowboat was very slow. But even though as Michael rowed, the sand and sludge would come up onto his oars, he continued to press on and pull and push at the waters that were in the front of him. Before long, the boat was floating into deeper water. They rode for about an hour watching the scenic views of the shorelines, which were inundated with rocks of every shade of the brown color. Mosses crept up to the shoreline and covered a lot of the ground. What looked like a line of green-colored lawn was easily spotted before the water's edge of the lake. Further in from the shoreline was the beginning of the mountains as rocks from the mountain dotted up and around the shoreline of the lake and further into the interior. Michael was on the lookout for an old, old pine tree that had drooping arms. He had strategically learned to identify it, and then he called to the young couple, and to the soldier who was with him, "hold on tight. The waters from here on change and soon we will come to a whirlpool. Do not be afraid. If we row very close to the shore, we will see the foaming waters from the whirlpool and we will avoid it". The young woman moaned. She caught her composure after a minute and asked, "Is there any other way of getting to a group of people?" Michael answered without hesitation, "Yes. There is another way, but you would have to go through a tunnel under the mountain. It is a safe way to go, but once, just once, the waters from river overflowed and we had to wait for a day or two for the waters to recede before going into the tunnel in the mountain. Michael assured the young couple that he knew what he was doing and that they would be safe. The young man interjected a thought, "But what if we walked by the shoreline?" he asked. Michael countered the young man's hesitation and said, "Oh, we can always find our way to the camp by following the shoreline, but the general idea is not to be out in the open. After all, we do not wish to become sitting or walking ducks for the Germans to pick us off one, two, and three".

Michael asked him, "Do you understand?" The young man bowed down his head and said, "Yes. I understand." The other soldier had been on the lookout for the whirlpool. He called out as he spotted the whirlpool, "There she blows. There she is, and immediately Michael's attention was on the whirlpool, and the young woman's eyes were glued to the chasing, and exploding waters, and the rising high waters as she clung to the shoulders of her husband. The young man's eyes were glued on the waters that were surrounding the boat. He was thinking of where to jump in the waters if the whirlpool started to pull the boat inside the whirlpool. They all were anxious, and the shine on the outside of their protruding eyes showed their feelings of fear. The sound of the rushing waters came closer and closer. There was a short silence as all of the waters in the whirlpool seemed to stop. Then came a loud rushing sound and one could see the water rising and one could hear the sound rising and rising to the top and beyond the top of the waters. A figure of a dragon with long, sharp talons on its long neck appeared to rise out of the waters of the lake. It rose higher and higher and looked like its entire width of its body and head of maybe 36 feet or more might jump out of the waters of the lake. The water's creature looked around the area of the lake with it large and extended, protruding green eyes. It snorted and let out fire from the tip of its tongue. Then it dived down deep into the waters of the lake, swishing and splashing with its scales on its body as it descended into the deep waters, which was murky water at the bottom of the lake and must have been over 50 feet deep. Michael, and the other partisan soldiers, and the young couple were both in awe and afraid of the creature. Michael told them all to calm down and that he had seen the creature many times before even though his own face was flushed. He said, "If we stick to the shore, the creature in the whirlpool does not see us and does not feel threatened by us". He paused, but breathed in a heavy breath, and said, "The water dragon is one of God's creatures, too."

The three angels and Anna were watching what was happening to the young couple. The female angel had set up a periscope in the interior of the cloud for everyone to watch what was happening. One of the male angels said to the female angel and to Anna, "Don't worry! If the angel thought that they were in danger, she would fly out to them and help them before the dragon got to them". Anna felt better about the situation, but she was quiet, and she was beginning to wonder when they would drive the cloud to take her home and let her go back into the bunker. She did not wish to tell the angels, but she was beginning to be tired even with her dogged determination to survive.

They raced with the waves of the lake, but stayed close to the shore. The other partisan was on the lookout for Nazis. Michael could see that the other partisan was concerned about the Nazis spotting them. He thought to himself, "Maybe this is an omen. Maybe we should bypass the entrance to the village that was hidden in the woods. Maybe they should ride further down the waves for another hour and then back track to the village through the woods. He said to the other soldier, "We will not stop. The Nazis could be watching us from any point on the mountains. Let us ride down the waters for at least an hour. Then we will back track and find the village through the wood. The other soldier agreed. They rode the waves up and down and bouncing, and Michael kept his pace with the oars. One of the oar tips went into the water as the other on the other side went into the waters at the same time. Then the oars were withdrawn from the water and then they went back in lifting waters back and forth. They had almost finished their journey when the other partisan spotted lights on the right side of the mountain. He spoke softly, but spoke into Michael's right ear. "They may have spotted us," he said. Michael countered with his thoughts, "If they haven't spotted us yet, they will soon. These lights tell us that they are signaling to each other. After the signals, one usually sees men in the distance coming down the pathway". The other partisan shuddered, but regrouped his composure and said, "I think that we have to stop the boat and pray. Then we will decide what to do". The young couple shuddered, but the man asked that they row to the shore and bring the boat up to the shore and secure it. He said, "I must pray for our lives". Michael said, "Yes", and he told the young man, "The fact that we are all here means that the angels are sent from G-d to protect us. They reached the shore. They all got out, and standing erect each of the four of them prayed to G-d for their lives. As they prayed, the Nazis began their march down the mountain into the woods.

❊   ❊   ❊

The Nazis Make An Attempt To Find The Village of Hidden People

Like the stroke of lightning, the pine trees that the Nazis passed extended their arms and grew to reach heights unheard of. The pine trees extended their arms to their sides and joined each other and blocked the Nazis from going any further. The Nazis tore at the branches of the pine trees and cut the branches down, and they continued like the devil continues and could not stop their pace and rage against the people in Slovakia. With their branches cut, the trees regrouped and sipped up the waters from within their systems and spit out the waters on the approaching Nazis. The waters from the pine trees contained a sap that was very sticky. The sap reached out and spilled all over their faces and the Nazis could not hear or see. They dropped their weapons. The weapons fell deep within the uncharted caverns of the mountains. Many of the soldiers dropped when they could not find their footing on the mountain ridges. One officer in charge yelled, "Regroup and continue". As he yelled, the sun shined brighter than ever on the pine trees on the mountains. The pine trees supped in the sun and their limbs grew. When the Nazi soldiers attempted to pass the mountains, they slapped the soldiers. When the soldiers wanted to fight back, they pushed the Nazi soldiers off of the ledges of the mountain ridges. They yelled as they were falling through the air. The echoes of the Nazis' voices resounded from mountain top to mountain top. Each time a Nazi soldier fell, he fell with a thud and he lay lifeless on the grounds that were never seen nor traveled before for centuries. Their bodies slowly seeped into the grounds. Birds flew over their bodies as their bodies were seeping into the ground. The birds landed and pecked at their faces. Bears came out of the deep, untraveled woods of rarely seen trees, and they leaped on the bodies of the Nazis and tore into their limbs with their beaks and carried carrion to their cubs to eat. The bears lived deep, deep into the hidden meadows and caves of the deep woods of Slovakia. Wolves raced down from the mountains in packs of six or eight or more and snarled at the bodies of the fallen Nazi soldiers and tore at their bodies and carried away carrion from their bodies. Echoes of their howls and their calls to each wolf could be heard in the distances from the echoes that resounded from the sounds. The people who were hidden in the village and in the caves could hear the resounding sounds. The partisans smiled with a feeling of peac for they knew what was happening. Michael said to his fellow soldier, "We are still not safe. The Nazis could send in other soldiers and they could send skiers to ski down the mountains. They could launch boats and travel down the river. They could send airplanes to shoot at us. We had better take to the woods. I know the way to the village. We have to travel due east, and we have to look for certain mountain ridges, which are markers.

❄   ❄   ❄

Michael and The Other Soldier Take the Young Couple to the Village

They docked the boat camouflaging it with branches from shrubs. They looked for landmarks that would help them to find the boat when they needed to return to this side of the woods. They covered the boat with many branches and shaped the branches so that the boat was completely camouflaged. Michael was the first to go into the woods. The partisan soldier followed and the young couple followed the partisan soldier. They entered what Michael termed as no man's land. The area was booby trapped with animal traps. This was done on purpose to catch Nazi invaders, but also to trap the bountiful supply of rabbits for food. Rabbit stew was the meal with black pepper, and lots of salt, and some well cooked white potatoes was the meal that they could rely upon. Anna was watching through the periscope and she envied the partisans. She thought that maybe she would tell Joseph to set some traps for rabbits. "Well", she said to herself, "It certainly would not hurt. It would not hurt a bit". She grew tired and had moments when she kept herself from trying to wake herself up. She was about to give in and fall asleep when the female angel pointed out to the other angels that Anna is tired and that they should be taking her back to the bunker.

The female angel steered the cloud to the left and then to the right and finally the cloud hovered on top of the bunker. The noise from the idling motor woke Anna. She awoke with a start. She realized quickly where she was. The female angel told her, "In moments we are going to land". Anna was so happy. The legs of the cloud moved down from the cloud and touched the base of the soil on the right side of the bunker entrance. The invisible door of the cloud swung open and Anna got out. She stood for a moment looking at the three angels and said thank you to them. She hesitated but then realized that she should ask the angels about food. Anna told the three angels, "I need food for dinner time when we are all in the bunker. The female angel said that Anna should turn around and look at the brown bear coming out of the woods. Anna was startled to see a brown bear, but she knew not to be startled or to be afraid, because the brown bear had a large grayling fish in its mouth. To Anna it looked like the bear was going to give her the grayling fish. Anna was right. The brown bear dropped the grayling fish near her feet and then in a short moment's time, the vision of the brown bear grew dimmer and dimmer. The bear simply turned around and ran away into the woods. She saw her son Martin looking for her, and she saw her son Bernard looking for her. As her sons came over to her, asking where she had been, the angels in the cloud took off for higher spheres in the sky. Anna said to Martin as she showed him the big grayling fish, "I was just near the other pine tree". She carried the grayling fish down the steps to the bunker with her. Martin announced to the family, "We are going to have a treat tonight. Everyone looked and everyone was pleased. Bernard was playing chess with Henry, but he looked up and said, "Good Ma". Anna got right to cutting up the fish and then throwing the fish into a hot pan that she warmed up on a fire that Joseph had made in the small oven that Joseph had built for his family. The fire in the oven also was used to heat the underground bunker. Anna passed out the pieces of fish on small pieces of cloth that she always washed in the early morning. It was her way of hoping that food would be available for the family on the next day. Anna sat in her hand-hewn chair and rocked herself. She closed her eyes, and she fell peacefully asleep. Joseph was glad that Anna was more relaxed. Joseph sat by her side for a long time and then slowly gave into sleep.

❋ ❋ ❋

The Angels Remain on Alert and Hover in the Cloud Over the Bunker

The female angel said to the other two angels, "I just do not know if we killed off all of the Nazis". One of the male angels said to her, "Let us park the cloud nearby and let us watch the bunker". They watched and they watched. Lights rotated in round circles a few miles near the bunker. All three of the angels saw the lights. One of the male angels quickly said, "It looks like a party of five or six soldiers walking in the dark. They are looking for someone or something in the dark. The lights that you see are from search lights. "It is best if I put the periscope down", said the female angel. The other two angels agreed. The angels watched the Nazi soldiers walking in the dark. "Wow", said one of the two male angels, "I wasn't quite sure who the people were, but now with the lenses on the periscope, I know for certain that we are looking at Nazis". The other man angel said, "You can bet that they are up to no good". "Sure thing", said the female angel. The three angels watched very carefully. Then one of the man angels said, "They are Nazi scouts. They are looking for a sneaky way into Micholovce. They are going to radio back to their base that they found a way through the woods and they are going to give the base the coordinates. Then the other male angel said, "We simply cannot allow them to continue". The female angel listened intently to her two brother angels and said, "I agree". She asked her brother angels, "What do you suggest we do?" One of the brother angels said, "We have to do a good job of getting rid of them. We want to send a message back to their command that they all disappeared and that it is dangerous to send out any other scouts. The other two angels agreed. The older of the two male angels said, "Leave this caper up to me". The other male angel agreed. The female angel agreed. Both the male and the female angels were curious to see what was going to happen. The two angels waited. The two angels watched.

The Nazi soldiers pushed forward into the deep hills, and bumps of land, and holes of the forest. The angel jumped up into a tree and shielded himself from the Nazi soldiers. He waited patiently, most patiently for the Nazis to walk under the tree. He waited and he panted.

Other than his breath blowing in the air and the glow from his emerald green-colored eyes, no one would ever imagine that he was lying in waiting to kill off the Nazis. The moment came. A Nazi soldier stepped on a branch and the branch crackled. That was the angel's clue. With his blacker than night color of his hair, he leaped with his four legs and one tale on the top of the Nazi soldier. The soldier yelled a yelping sound, which alerted Joseph. The yelping sound alerted all of the other creatures in the woods. The owl who posited herself on a tree branch from a tree across from this one, hooted louder and louder. She sounded the alarm for all of the forest animals to be on the alert for the killer Nazis. Rats who came out of their burrows during the night to prowl through the wild grasses realized that their territory was being invaded and they leaped for the closed refuge.

The panther lay on top of the soldier. He leaped for the soldier's neck and with the whitest teeth in the forest, bit into the throat of the Nazi soldier. The Nazi soldier squirmed, but the air from his body seeped out into the air, and the blood from his wound poured onto the ground and he succumbed quickly. The next soldier grappled in the dark, hardly being able to discern who killed his comrade. He pulled out his revolver and aimed at the black figure, but the black figure disappeared and all of his bullets were spent.

Joseph woke up Anna and told her that she and Edith and the boys were to go quickly to the back of the bunker. They all left for the back of the bunker without asking any questions. Joseph followed quickly behind them. Joseph thought to himself, "It is a good thing that we have a plan to escape from the back of the bunker. My goodness, who would ever think that the Nazis would come in the dark of night?"

The second Nazi soldier realized that all of his bullets were gone. Seeing that the bullets were all spent, the black panther ran faster than the speed of light and leaped onto the throat of the second soldier. He bit into the fibers of the sinews of the Nazi's neck. The Nazi chocked on his own blood and fell to his knees and then fell on his face, lying where he would never again rise to kill innocent people. Four more Nazis sprang towards the black creature of the night, but the panther eluded them. They aimed their revolvers. Each shot at a black figure in the night that they thought was the panther, but not one of their bullets met its mark. They spent their bullets. The panther leaped on the last of the soldiers from the back and bit into his spine and the man fell forward, dead before he reached the ground. The panther leaped on the next soldier that was left in line, and he jumped on his back, and covered the Nazi's eyes and pulled at the soldier's eyes until the claws of his strong paws tore out the Nazi's eyes. The panther bit into his spine and pulled off a piece of the spine. The Nazi screamed so loud that the echoes resounded, and resounded back and forth, and the echoes did not know when to stop resounding. The panther disappeared. The two Nazis ran through the woods. One stumbled. One soldier stopped to catch his breath. The surrounding trees came closer and closer to them, forming a circle around them. The Nazis had nowhere to go, but they lashed out at the trees. The roots of the trees felt anger and oozed out of the ground and reached out like cobras encircling their victims and strangled them. The roots threw the bodies of the two soldiers up in the air and the bodies fell flat on the trunks of the trees. The trunks opened up their doors and swallowed up the Nazis. The Nazis disappeared and remained in oblivion forever. They were thrown into a third world in which their punishment was to float through the air for the rest of their lives.

A figure of a panther appeared and then turning one time around changed into the figure of an angel. The angel flew up to the cloud and the cloud let him in immediately. The female angel and the other male angel both praised the male angel for his bravery. As they were talking, they heard a beep, beeping sound, and they knew that the sound was from a transmission. The female angel got back into her seat and said to the two other angels, "Quickly, let us intercept this transmission. Let us find out what is happening". The other angels agreed. The female angel pressed the button and the picture from the radio frequency circled in red on the screen and beeped transmission sounds softly. The female angel said "Soon the beep is going to be louder, and when the red line on the picture stops rotating, and the beep is loud, I will press the green button, and we will be able to hear every word that is said. They waited for the loud beeping sound and soon the sound got louder. They watched for the red line in the screen to stop and it stopped. The female angel pressed the green button, and they listened to the transmission as the voices said, "It is the base. Come in. Come in. Should I send in more men? I want to send in 10 more men, would that do?" the voice at the other end of the transmission asked. Then the same voice yelled,

"Answer me. Answer me". There was no answer. Then the voice yelled, "I will send you 10 more men, and I will send them immediately", and then the transmission ended.

"Okay", said the female angel to the other two angels. "We have to decide whether or not we should call in for more angel reinforcements." One male angel answered, "It will not be necessary. I will tell you what to do". He said, "Listen to me and we will fare well. You have to divide up the cloud in three pieces. Each one of us will drive a cloud separately and will have the weapons to fight these ten men. We will keep our transmissions open to each other all the time. No one is to leave their cloud for we might not be able to help if we are no longer a part of a big cloud".

The male angel said, "I hear those men coming. The Nazis are coming over the ridge. Listen to me and do exactly what I tell you to do". The other two angels listened. The male angel continued, "I am going to ask all of the trees on this side of the forest to donate one branch each". No sooner did the male angel say that when each tree in a circumference of 100 feet donated a branch by dropping a big size branch onto the ground.

The male angel waved his finger in the air and the branches that had just fallen off the trees got up and saluted to the male angel. The male angel said, "Good". He commanded the branches to follow his orders. He said that he wanted to make a large raft with one-third of the branches. He continued by saying that he wanted the rest of the branches to fall into formation and become a fence. The branches fell into formation and in seconds they become a formidable fence. The remainder of the branches remained on the ground and waited for their orders.

Onwards and up the hills in the mountains the Nazis marched. One by one they marched. It was almost nightfall when they reached the fence. One Nazi soldier raised his hand and said, "Halt". He told another soldier to throw a grenade at the fence. The soldier threw a grenade at the fence. The grenade almost landed on the fence, but it stopped in mid air about three feet from the fence and the grenade rotated and turned around completely and then aimed at the Nazi soldiers. The Nazi soldiers ran for cover. All but one soldier escaped. The grenade exploded near him and that was the end of him. The Nazi soldier fell flat on the ground from the thud. He would never get up again. The nine Nazi soldiers regrouped. One of the soldiers spotted the raft and said, "There must be a river or lake nearby and we can float on this raft". The commanding officer said, "I will allow six men to carry the raft to the nearby lake and to set the raft down on the lake". The other two men will come with me. The men carried the raft, but as it was very heavy, and they decided to put it down on the ground for a while they caught their breath. They breathed in and out many times. One soldier even leaned down holding his knees as he breathed in heavily. It was at just that moment in time that the raft began to talk. The men listened to what the raft had to say even though their eyes protruded as they listened most carefully to what the raft had to say. The raft said to the soldiers, "I can fly". And then the raft gave good advice, "Why carry me when you do not have to carry me?" Then the raft gave more advice, "Come aboard, and I will lift you into the air, and we will fly across the whole forest". The six men were still tired and weary from carrying the raft. They got onto the raft thinking it was a good idea and the raft lifted them up, and they were flying. They were so happy. They passed over the commanding Nazi soldier and his two comrades and as they did, they waved. The commanding officer yelled at them to get down, saying, "dumb kup" come down, but the raft told them that they were in for a treat and so the soldiers were happy that they were going to get a treat. They flew away quickly from the officers and the two other soldiers, leaving them in the middle of the woods. They were surrounded by trees. They had lost their direction. The officer spotted a mountain top and called to the other two soldiers, "Come. This is the way to the Tatra Mountains.

The raft continued to fly around the forest tree tops. The raft said that he was going to show them some people who were living in the woods. The raft swooped and looped around the industrious trees. The raft took the six men above the lake and into the air above the mountains. When they reached a cave that was hidden on the side of one of the mountains, the raft stopped flying around, and floated, and circled in the air. The men looked all around to see anyone or anything in the cave, but held on for dear life onto the edges of the raft.

The raft said to them, "Look to the right of the entrance in the cave". And the raft asked, "What do you see?" One of the men on the raft shouted, "I do not see anyone or anything". The raft hovered over the entrance of the cave. Another one of the soldiers shouted, "I see an old man and a younger man". The raft's voice spoke as it asked the question, "What do you think is happening to the older man and the young son?" The soldier shook his head and said, "I do not know". The raft insisted that the men on the raft look at the man as he said to the men, "Which of you can face the truth? Tell me what is going to happen to the old man and to his young son?" One of the soldiers answered, "He will probably die of hunger or from the cold". "Yes", said the raft, "You have answered my question finally". "Now said the raft, who was really one of the two male angels from the cloud, "What would you do to save the old man and the young man?" Not one of the German soldiers could answer the question. "Then I will tell you", said the raft. "Look closely at me and listen at what I tell you to do." The soldiers laughed as the raft sped away from the opening of the cave and looped around, and about, and came back to the opening. The raft asked the same question over again, "What would you do to save the old man and the young man?" One of the soldiers answered, "I would drop down some food". "Oh", said the raft. "That sounds good, but how would you know that the old man and the young man would get the food?" The soldier did not know how to answer and just shook his head. The raft's voice began to sound agitated and called out loudly to the men, "Would you bring the food to the men?" The soldiers stammered, and they cleared their throats, but they could not answer. The raft then asked them in a steel, cold calm voice, "If I gave you the food to bring to the old man and the young man, would you bring the food to them?" The soldier's laughed. "Then you are as wicked as your leaders are", shouted the raft and the sounds of his words echoed and resounded from one mountain top to the other. "Well then you shall be food yourselves for some of the giant fish in the lake," and a huge wave of air blew against the men and as hard as they tried to hold onto the raft, the force of the air pulled their hands away from holding onto the edges of the raft. The men's fingers gave way and they lost their grip and could not hold onto the raft. Their bodies rolled down the declining descent of the raft.

Each one of the men flew with the waves of air, and circled up, and down, and around, but descended straight downwards ultimately in a matter of minutes into the deep blue waters of the lake. As they fell into the water, there was an enormous burst of white waters flying high into the air. The raft flew above them and watched the scene and saw the enormous force of the waters as the waters resisted their intrusion. Great swells of white foaming waters could be seen reaching up high into the air and almost reaching the sky. As the foams reached their crests and then finally descended, they covered up the opening in the waters where each of the men had fallen. There was no trace of the men. There was nothing left that remained of the men.

The male angel who was disguised as the raft saw the six men swallowed up by the lake waters. The raft slowly began to change into a figure of a white outline. As minutes passed, the white outline filled and the body of the angel in the shape of a man could easily be discerned. The angel said to himself, "I will bring food and water to the old man and to the young man. The angel searched the waters for fish. He waited for a grayling fish to surface and it was not long before a grayling fish ascended in a straight line up from the murkiness of the waters into the pristine, clear waters of the top of the lake water. "Wow, this is a big fish", shouted the angel and he flew to the entrance of the cave and dropped down with the fish to the ground. The angel pretended that he was a local hunter and that he was just passing by with a big fish and happened to see the old man and the young man. The angel brought the two men in the cave the fish and also like magic, big mushrooms appeared on the floor on one side of the cave. "There", he said to the young man and the old man, "you will always have nourishment. The hunter pretended he was looking for another way out of the cave and he soon felt the cave's inner walls. He pressed his ears close by to the walls of the cave and when he heard a gurgling sound, he said, "Aha", and he pressed his hand firmly onto the wall and a small stream of mountain water flowed into the cave. "There", he called out to the old man and to the young man, "there are mushrooms growing on the floors of the cave. There is fish in the nearby lake, and now you shall have fresh water running down the walls of the cave. The old man said, "Thank you. You are an angel from heaven. The hunter blushed and said to the old man, "I am just a hunter who looks after people who need a little bit of help". The old man and the young man smiled.

The hunter said that he would be going and he was about to leave, but he turned around and said, "Make a wish for the Christmas and maybe your wish will come true". The two men smiled and agreed. The hunter turned towards the forest and in moments, he disappeared into the colors, tones of the earth. There was no distinguishing him from the trees that he passed quickly by. The old man and the young man would forever remember the hunter, and they would talk about the hunter between themselves for many years to come. The thought of receiving help revived the two men, and they began to talk and make plans about surviving the war. The hunter was actually heading back to his cloud. He walked briskly into the heart of the woods, but then there was a clearing where trees that fallen had lain for a long, long time. The male angel rotated his finger clockwise for five times and his personal cloud appeared. He flew up to the cloud and got in quickly, driving away from the woods and heading to the dock where the other two angels were waiting to welcome him into the big cloud.

"Well, welcome back to our home, said the female cloud to the male angel. The other male angel smiled, and nodded his head, and he squinted his left eye and raised his left thumb into the air. "Big job", said the male angel. He hesitated and said, "I gave those men a chance to redeem themselves, but they could not understand the concept of doing good for people". The female angel nodded her head and said, "You tried to teach those men the right way to behave. You can only lead them to the right direction. They have to do the right thing by themselves". "Well", said the male angel, "At least I tried to show them the right way". There was silence. They all sat quietly. They sat for a while, and the peace, and quiet was good for them. The female angel interrupted the quiet by asking a question, "How is it that we have so much work to do against evil and there are only a few of us?" "Good question", responded the male angel. "I think that I know the answer", he said. The other male angel listened intently. The female angel had an expression of intense concentration on her face. The male angel explained in a calm and quiet sounding voice, "We are few because G-d has chosen us from the men of the living who have distinguished themselves for their goodness. As you know there are four types of people. There are those who are genuinely good people and do good all of their lives. There are those who wish to do good, but somehow never get the opportunity to do good. There are those who question the deeds of others and yet cannot do as well themselves. There are the bad, evil people who do not wish to change their evil habits". "Oh", said the female angel, "Now that you have explained this to me, I think that I understand better". The other male angel said, "I agree".

There was a beeping sound from the transmitter and the female angel responded by pressing the acknowledgement button. "Let me see what the transmitter is trying to tell us". The three angels huddled closely together and watched the picture come onto their vision set, which was in a wide circle on the dashboard with the other controls in the front of the cloud. They saw the three remaining Nazi soldiers on the screen, and they could hear them. The angels listened most carefully to what the three Nazi soldiers were saying. The leader, the officer in charge, was talking, and he was quite vociferous in his mannerisms. "We must find people who are hiding in the woods. That is our mission", he said, and we shall do it". The other two soldiers agreed. The three men marched on into the woods.

The female angel asked the other two angels, "Should I intercept them or do you wish to deal with them?" One of the male angels suggested as he nodded his head in an expression of disgust, "Let us watch them very carefully". Then the second male angel said, "When you feel that I should go after the three Nazis, I will do so". The other two angels agreed. The three angels watched the screen intently.

The three Nazis continued their trek through the woods as they walked through a pathway that was covered partially in snow with some sections were of ice on the surface of the snow. The roughness of the terrain halted their way along the trail as they had to go around the spots of icy terrain. Rabbits darted in front of them unaware of their presence at first, but when the rabbits realized that they were threatened, they hopped over the ice and hastened to find their burrows. The officer in charge said, "I think that I hear some noise". He stopped. The two men stopped. He listened. One of the men meekly said, "It must be the rabbit that I just saw". "No", said the officer, "It sounds like someone is behind the bushes near us and not like a rabbit is running". The two men nodded. They listened for the sound. It was a rustling sound that was coming through the brambles, patches of bushes that were just ahead of them.

The officer motioned to the two men to crouch down. They did crouch down and lie on the cold, bitter cold ground. They lay in wait. The fear of whatever it was that was making the noise worked on their feelings of fear. Their thoughts were inundated with guesses and assumptions for whatever creature would come out of the brambles of bushes. Slowly but surely a white looking creature emerged in plain sight, leaving the brambles of bushes behind him.

The animal was not a young creature for he was a big size. He had horns that were well formed and protruded from his forehead about nine inches. This animal knew his way through the woods and had a built-in location device that told him what was north and south of him and told him what was west and east of him. It was not that he seemed to follow a trail. The expression on his face was a serious one. The animal knew moment to moment where he was even though he was surrounded by trees that inched up towards the sky and crowded the forest floor with more and more trees every year. There were mountain ridges that looked similar in size, and shape, and color, but were entirely different, and the goat knew all of this.

"Oh", said the officer, "Follow this goat and we will find some people hiding in the woods". The goat went on his way down and up the trails but descended mostly downwards along the rocky trail that was sometimes blocked by a fallen tree. The goat picked up his pace as if to sense that someone or something was lurking in the forest that was not friendly. The goat had a habit of stopping along the trail and looking around the trail. The officer and the men picked up their pace also, but it was difficult to follow a goat. The goat was more agile on the mountain terrain. The goat knew the trail, because it had been a trail that many goats followed.

The officer and the men soon grew weary as they followed the goat up the mountains and then down the mountain trails. "Where is this goat going?" asked the officer. One of the men shrugged his shoulders. After a while, the three men grew weary and the officer asked, "Should I shoot the goat?" And the men did not know how to answer, and they shrugged their shoulders. The officer shouted, "Dumb, dumb", at the two soldiers, and he took out his pistol and aimed at the goat as assuredly as he had aimed his words to pierce the emotions of his two soldiers. The goat had taken a route that was becoming completely downhill. Then unexpectedly, it turned sharply to the right and headed through a thin crevice in a gigantic boulder on the edge of the mountain.

The bullet that was aimed hit the sides of the mountain, and the echoes resounded round, and round, and about the mountain tops, and down the mountain, and up the mountain until the bullet splattered in hundreds of pieces. The sound of the piercing bullet could be heard for miles and miles away from the mountain. People in the nearby village heard the resounding echoing sounds. Then as the shattering sounds abated, there was complete silence.

The Nazi officer held onto his ears tightly as the noise resounded. The two soldiers followed his example and held onto their ears tightly and pressing their hands inwards towards the centers of their ears, they could hardly hear anything. The Nazi officer said to the soldiers, "I have to rest. I have to take off my left boot." He sat down, and pulled off his boot, and felt the toe. He moaned out loud as he touched his big toe for the toe hurt, "That damn goat. Why did I follow him? I just do not know". He sat for a long time on the ground and when the pain in his toe abated, the officer got up. He proceeded to walk down a trail. The two soldiers followed his every move. This trail led down the mountain and led to a village that was located in the valley of the mountain. It was a small farming village. The town had long since been established for generations and generations. Everyone knew each other. Most people had grown up in the village, and had stayed, and married, and raised their families and farmed. Most of the people in the village stayed for their entire lifetime. It was a pleasant village with large size homes that were covered on the outside with the many stones that had been dug up from the ground in the village. Wooden, thatched roofs covered the structures of the homes securely. Each home had a large size fireplace that practically covered the entire side of the home.

A large church had been built in the middle of the town. The church's priest was revered and had always helped as many people as he could. There was an assistant priest who always worked hand-in-hand with him to help the people of the town. Together, they helped a lot of people. The two Priests extended their benevolence to help people hiding in the woods. It meant no difference to them if the people hiding in the woods were Jews. They openly declared that it was the will of G-d and the will of Christ to help these unfortunate people. Many of the families in the village had taken in children from Jewish homes and had raised the children as their own. No one talked about this, because they were afraid of the Nazi reprisal. They, nevertheless, did their very best to help the innocent victims of the war.

❄ ❄ ❄

The Officer and The Two Soldiers Continue Their Trek Through The Woods

There was a decided chill in the air. The three men continued their trek through the woods. The three men continued with their force and threat to commit wrongful acts against innocent people. The officer, however, was not able to continue much further through the woods. His big toe was swollen, and he was beginning to feel sharp pains shooting up into his legs. Soon the whole foot began to ache. When this happened, he ordered that the two soldiers stop, and he sat down on the ground. He pulled off his boot. He pulled off the heavy sock that was covering his foot. He twisted his foot so that he could feel the circulation in it. He looked most carefully at his big toe. He exclaimed, "Yow. It is swollen". The two officers just looked on and said not a word. The officer looked up at them while tilting his face and looked like he was looking for an excuse to yell at the two officers. Each of the two officers knew that he was looking for an excuse to yell, and they were smart enough not to give him an excuse. The two soldiers stood mute for at least an hour. The officer declared, "I am going to stay here for a while, and he asked, "Can you go down to the villager by yourselves? The two men instantly responded by saying, "yes". "Find a place to take off your uniforms and walk around like you are hunters who are coming into the village to stay for the night". The officer hesitated and then questioned, "Do you think that you can do that without me?" Both soldiers immediately answered, "Oh, yes". "Well then go. I will find you, and I will contact you.

Now go". The two men went. They walked briskly along the trail. When they had gone a significant distance, the taller one said to the shorter one, "I think we got a lucky break". The shorter one smiled and laughed. They both laughed, and they walked down the downhill path that led to the town. It took them about two hours or a little more time, but they made to the village. They stopped at the very edge of the village and both looked with a puzzled expression on their faces. They did not know where to go. They did not know what house to knock on. They stood for a while looking at the town. Then the taller realized that they had to get rid of their uniforms first. The shorter one said, "There is a farm just to the right not far from here. We might be able to find some clothes hanging on a clothes line". The shorter one was right. There were a lot of men's pants, and underwear, and shirts, and undershirts hanging on the line. They buried their uniforms and put on plenty of shirts and found pants that fit and were on their merry way. It was almost dark out. They had grown hungry. They looked for the nearest barn where they might find some food. They were about to open the doors of the barn, when the family dog spotted them and yelped and howled. The owner of the house came out with a shot gun. He said, "What brings you men here to my house?" The big soldier hesitated and cleared his throat. He nodded for the shorter one to answer. The shorter one did not hesitate with his answer. He said that they were hunters who lived in the woods. They were following a deer and came to this part of the woods". He continued, "A robber came out of the bushes and robbed them of their money. The robber took their jackets and they are just coming to the barn to sleep, and to get warm, and to find some food". "Oh", said the farmer, as he stood in astonishment that a robber in these parts could be so bad a person. He said immediately, "I can bring you some plates of rabbit stew, and pieces of pie, and some coffee to wash down the food". The taller man said immediately, "Thank you for your kindness". The farmer left the barn, but was back in a half hour. His fourteen year old son was with him. His son carried a large pot of rabbit stew, and he brought two bowls and two spoons, and two large cloth napkins for them to wipe their hands with. The father brought the two men two jackets and he said, "These two jackets have been lying around in the closet forever and it is time that someone had a use from wearing them," he said. The two men said, "thank you" at the exact time. Both men smiled, and the farmer, and his son walked back to their house. They were proud that they had helped two men who had been in distress.

❄   ❄   ❄

The Two Men Spend The Night In The Farmer's Barn

"Oh, look here at all this meat", said the shorter one". The taller one laughed as he grabbed his bowl, and spoon, and spooned out a large portion of the rabbit meat and potatoes. He sat down on a haystack and in moments he was licking his tongue after every bit. With a mouth full of food, he declared, "This stew is mighty good. Yup. Mighty good". The shorter one smiled and ate the pieces of rabbit stew and shook his head as he declared, "Yes. This stew is mighty good. Mighty good". They both laughed and kicked their legs as though they were dancing as they scooped in the food into their mouths. When they were done eating, they rested on the haystacks where they were sitting. Neither man could get up for a while. Finally, the shorter man declared, "I am going to cover myself with my jacket and he lay down on the barn floor and before long, he was in a deep slumber. The taller one reached for his jacket and lay down on the floor. He fell away fast asleep. Each man slept soundly until the light from the new day crept into the window.

They both woke up a bit startled, shaking their heads many times, and they both looked at each other with wide-open eyes. The taller one said to the shorter one, "I just do not know about this war?" The shorter one asked, "Why is it that you say that?" "Well, there is so much kindness amongst these peoples. I just do not know what to believe". The shorter one asked, "Oh, why is that?" The taller one replied, "We, all of us have been taught to kill and to kill, yet these people give food to strangers, and they give their clothing to us". "You are right. These are good people. They are all good people. I begin to question why we are here. I begin to question why the German Army is raging war and killing good people". The shorter man hesitated, and he grimaced for a minute, and said in a soft tone of voice, "I am beginning to think that you are right, but you must never tell anyone else what you believe. It is much too dangerous for us". The taller man said, "But we were sent here to spy on these people and to find out who is hiding Jews". The shorter one hesitated and said, "Let us just play it cool. Remember we are just hunters who have lost our way. Have to play it safe, otherwise the Nazis will kill us for certain". The taller one said, "The Nazis cannot kill us for something that we do not know. Stick with me on this issue. I do not want to kill anyone. I do not want to kill anyone anymore. I want to go home to my family and enjoy peace. The shorter one hesitated for a moment and then mumbled, "I feel the same way. I just do not wish to have any more blood on my hands, no more. No more". The taller one said, "Then you must listen to what I tell you to do for I will tell you to do only good, and you must follow me". The shorter man replied, "I will do so, but quietly".

They got up, dusted off their clothing, and were about to go their way, when the taller one said to the shorter one, "Do you think that we could knock on their door and ask them for some breakfast?" The shorter one hesitated and looked the taller one right in the eye, but then backed down saying, "Oh, all right. It is better to ask them than to go searching for some food". The taller one knocked on the farmer's door. A young woman about 26, but with real beauty that defined her personality for her good thoughts, opened the door and told the two men to come into the house. She led them through a long hallway and then into a huge size kitchen that was built in the back of the house. She pointed to the large kitchen table which was uncovered, but had a very large bowl and it was filled with apples, and pears, and grapes. She pointed with her hand for the men to sit down. They pulled out their chairs from under the table very quickly. They breathed in heavily for they were excited and anxious to participate in a meal with people. The taller soldier was thinking, "No more shooting and killing people". The shorter soldier was thinking, "No more spying on people". They both sat quietly and folded their hands on the table. The farmer's wife brought two full plates laden with food and placed them before the men on the table. The taller man stuck his fork immediately into five large fried potatoes. Then he dug his fork into a large mound of scrambled eggs. He reached for one of the hot biscuits on the edge of his plate and almost swallowed the entire biscuit in one time. The younger man slurped up some of the hot coffee and reached for a spoonful of eggs. The young woman watched the two men eat and she smiled. In ran a young boy with a large size dog behind him and behind the dog ran another boy, a year or two older than his brother. "Are you here for breakfast?" asked the young woman. "Yes", answered the two young sons instantly and at the same time. The dog, which was a mutt and was the size of any medium sized dog, barked his answer of affirmation. Their mother put a plate before them each, as they quickly both pulled out their chairs, scratching the wood surface on the floor of the kitchen as they tugged at their chairs. The young boys looked with a serious expression on their faces, looked at their mother questioningly, but she nodded and pointed her finger for them not to ask any questions. The boys ate their breakfast quietly but the expressions on their faces expressed their concern.

About a half hour later, the farmer and his older son walked in through the kitchen door. "We have hunters who have come to our house as guests", he announced as he smiled knowing that they were eating with him and his family. The farmer and his older son sat down. The farmer's wife put plates that were filled with fried potatoes and scrambled eggs before them. The farmer and his son slurped down the food and drank the hot cups of coffee, which were doused with milk. They ate so fast that they were breathing heavy. When the farmer was done eating, he announced, "I wish to officially present to you my two guests, and he waved his hands at the men. The taller man introduced himself as Rolph and the shorter man introduced himself as Jon. They all nodded. The farmer's wife took out a hot apple pie from the oven. She cut the pie into pieces. She passed out pieces to all of the men. She took a plate of fried potatoes and scrambled eggs and sat down at the table and ate heartily. The farmer talked. There are people who are starving in the woods and who need our help. Everyone listened. "The older boy, Josh, and I are going to be attending a meeting with many of the other men in town at the church". He asked Rolph and Jon, "Would you like to come along?" They both hesitated for a moment, and then both said at the same time, "Okay. We would like to come". They both bowed their heads. Seeing the humility on the two men's faces, the farmer announced, "We must say a prayer for peace". Each man and the farmer's wife bowed their heads and prayed silently. When they were done, they all said, "Amen". The farmer announced, "The meeting is at the church, and we are to be there this evening at 7pm. Walk so that no one sees you". The farmer got up from the table, and thanking his wife for the delicious breakfast, he and his oldest son, Josh walked briskly into the fields. The taller man and the shorter man walked into the fields too.

❄   ❄   ❄

The Lone Officer Finds Help

He had sat for a long time on the huge boulder that lay near the side of the trail. He had even fallen asleep while sitting on the rock. He reckoned with himself, "Have to get up soon, and find some food, and shelter. He was able to stand now for the throbbing in his big toe had stopped. He looked over the mountains, seeking a good place of refuge, using his eyes as a periscope. He was searching for a building that would be placed somewhere in the middle of the woods that he could stay for a few days. He looked and he looked. He could not discern even a small cottage in the woods. He sat down on the boulder. He thought that he would wait for a little while and then get up and look again more carefully. About an hour's time passed him by. There was no noise. It was serenely quiet where he was sitting on a boulder near the pathway down a mountain. He heard a faint noise. The noise got louder and louder.

He tried to discern what the noise could be. He thought, "It sounds like someone walking down a nearby pathway. He tried to find where the noise was coming from. Before his very eyes, he saw a man with a cap and a leather jacket walking down a nearby path. He thought, "That man is no danger to me, but maybe I can find out if he lives in a house in the woods. This time he looked up the mountain to the side of him. He said to himself, "If the man is going downhill, he had to come from someplace that was uphill, and maybe nearby. He searched and he searched. A large falcon bird flew over the horizon. He was curious about the bird. He watched the bird most carefully and then it disappeared somewhere on the tops of the trees. He said to himself, "I must walk in the direction that the bird was flying in. It must have been looking for water. If I find the water, then I will find the hunter's cabin. He walked on the trail towards where the bird could no longer be seen.

He walked and he walked. He knew, however that he was going in the right direction. He started to see a large space amongst the trees as he walked on. He limped at times, but he walked on. There was a breeze in the air and the air brought the scent of pristine, pure water into its mist. Before long, he discovered where the body of water was located. It was a lake that had formed hundreds and hundreds of years before. There was no telling that only a few people had ever discovered the waters of the land. Its water had the essence of a mist around it. Its waters in the middle were translucent and one could easily see schools of fish swimming beneath the surface of the water. The grayling fish swam up to the surface of the water and blew their bubbles and then dived down into the deep waters. The water was steel blue and very pure. The pure waters secured a nurturing habitat for the many sizes and shapes of fish that spawned in the waters. The grayling fish was not only abundant, but thrived in these same waters. Water was the source of life for the animal habitat in the waters of the lake. The water was the source of life for people hiding in the woods. Anna and Joseph as well as Martin, Sam, Bernard, Henry, and their daughter Edith came to the waters of the lake for water and fish. They came to collect some of the algae in the waters for food. They came to cut the wild grasses to serve as greens to serve with the grayling fish. The water was also a sense of peace and purity for the Freier family. The waters were untouched by the war. The water was their haven. They almost forgot to be on the lookout for Nazi soldiers. The waters were so soothing to their spirits.

The Nazi Officer Continues His Trek

It was not long before the Nazi officer discovered where the mystery of the cabin was located. It was built propped up against a mountain ridge at the other end of the lake. The image of a small cabin caught his eye as his eyes followed the long edges of the lake round and round and about. The cabin had been built by the hunter. The hunter had felled down the trees. The hunter had split the logs and nailed the pieces of wood together where needed on the structure of the house. He nailed the shingles on the roof by himself. He had included two windows in the house. The windows were built on the sides of the house. The Nazi officer huffed and puffed as he made his way to the cabin door. He reached for the handle of the front door as though he was using his last bit of strength, and he pulled down the latch, and the latch gave way. The door opened with a start and a long, extended creaking sound. He pushed himself into the cabin. His first vision of the inside of the cabin was of neatness. Everything that his eyes spotted was very neat. He looked for the kitchen and in a moment's time he spotted pots hanging from a rack in the middle of the kitchen. He opened one of the draws to the cupboard, and he found fresh bread, which had only one end piece cut off.

The soldier cut off a piece of the bread. He remarked to himself as he chewed the bread briskly, if only I had some jam to put onto the bread. He thought to himself, "With the jam, the bread is delicious". He reached for the top cupboard draw where he hoped that there would be jam and he found some strawberry jam. He put the jam onto the bread and sat down and he shook his head as he devoured one piece of bread after the other. He was finished eating when the bread was all gone. He was still hungry. He opened up another cupboard draw and found cans of sardines. He opened up one of the cans and lifted the sardines to his mouth and swooped the fish into his mouth and down his throat in one full motion—just like a whale swallowing up a smaller fish. He was still hungry. He searched the draws and found some small honey cakes. He put five of the small cakes in his big hand and then one by one he bit into the cakes until the cakes were gone. He said to himself, "I feel full". He sat down on one of the kitchen chairs and reached for a hot cup of coffee and a mug that was placed neatly on top of the stove. He poured the coffee until the top of the cup was filled to the brim. He sat down while leaning on the back of the chair and sipped one small sip after another of the hot freshly brewed coffee. He was at peace with himself. He slowly slipped into a deep sleep. He slept the rest of the afternoon away. It was almost dark when he awoke, and he awoke with a start. He knew that he must be going. He followed with his eyes the lights from the nearby town and descended down the mountain. As he came to the town, he saw people going into the church. His clothes were all changed so he looked like a hunter so he had no fear of entering the church. He followed the other men and women and sat down amongst them in the church.

Making Plans For Christmas At The Church

The church was located almost exactly in the middle of the village. It was built many, many years before in the middle of town. Slowly the area around the town expanded as more and more people chose to live in the village. When there were enough people in the town, they all built the church together. The Catholic Church, this church, was a rather large building, all white on the outside, and the outside was built with large stones and the foundation of the building was built with even larger stones. The steeple seemed to stand out higher than any other church's steeple. The steeple reached high up into the sky. It was the glow of the light from the cross that radiated above the mountain peaks and along the many mountain paths. An old man in his 80's climbed the stairwell every day to ring the bell every morning in time for the morning mass and after dinner time for the nightly mass. The cross of Christ was more visible than in most other churches because of this radiating light. Even though most of the inhabitants of the town were poor people, the cross had been molded out of pure gold. When the sun shined down on the valley, the vision of the cross shined upon all of the mountain tops.

This town was also seen and known by people as the sounds of horse's hooves, and the hammering on walls and roofs, and sounds of fixing barns, and the sounds of threshing and clicks of the gathering the crops, and the sounds of the rough winds that once in a while echoed, and resounded back, and forth and onwards from one mountain peak to the other. There was the sense of motion in this town. Everyone was busy. Everyone was occupied with a task. There was a strong sense of appreciation of work by the people. There was a strong sense of G-d in the people in the town. It was rumored from generation to generation that angels from high up above watched over the people in the town. Together with the sounds of the echoes and the illumination of the light, the surrounding woods and mountains were colored with natural hues of brown, and greens, and blues, and purples that visiting the town were like visiting G-d's country.

Many of the mountains had never been explored. The mountains retained their natural beauty and warmth for hundreds and hundreds of years. It was as though God's generosity had preserved the inside of the valley and had also preserved the surrounding areas outside of the boundaries of the town. It had always been whispered amongst the people that angels lived in clouds high up above the town. No one really believed the stories of G-d's angels, but it was nice to talk about once and a while. When the war came, the Priests from the church organized the people to resist the Nazis, but did so in the most tacit of ways. The people were encouraged to follow the ways of G-d always and to pray for peace.

The big-size front doors of the church were always open all day and all night. Many a person seeking refuge from surrounding towns found their way to the church and were helped with food and housing.

The people from the town came into the church for the meeting. The church had many chairs in the main room, but the Priest motioned that everyone should follow him down a long crescent-shaped stairway that led to a bottom floor hallway and the hallway led to a large hall. There were many chairs to sit on in this hall. There must have been over 50 chairs. One by one the feet of the men stamped the stairwell one step at a time as they went into the poorly lit bottom floor. The sounds of their footsteps reverberated into the history of the building and brought meaning to the building. One man amongst them was dressed like the farmers, and walked like the farmers, and talked like the farmers, but was not one of the farmers. He was not interested in serving the cause of the people. He was not ready to listen to the Priest. He was not able to distinguish between what was wrong and what was right.

The Priest called out, "No need for much of your time. This will be a quick meeting. An elderly man came from a room on the side of the hall and brought in a well-lit candle lamp. The Priest said, "Thank you Max. We shall now have the additional light". The Priest said as he crossed his chest, "Let us all say a silent prayer for the mission that we are about to embark on. All of the men and the few women that had come all prayed fervently. They all knew that the stakes were high. They all knew that they had to do something against the subversive Nazis. They all prayed and then the Priest said, "In the name of the Father, and the Holy Ghost, Christ wants us to help those people who are starving out in the woods". He paused and then he said, "Christ wants us to extend our hands and our good fortune to these unfortunate people". All of the people in the crowd said out loud the word, "Amen". The people in the crowd lifted up their heads. They felt renewed with their purpose.

The Priest paused as he stepped up closer to the front of the room, looked at everyone at one time, and stepped back a few paces closer. He swiftly faced the crowd of people as he stood firmly on his feet, and he asked as he started to count, "How many of us are here?" He called out the numbers as he counted the men sitting in the chairs. One two, three, four, five, six and he reached the number 55 men very swiftly. Every man felt good about being counted as one could see the smiles on their faces. The Priest announced, "As you probably all know the war is worse, and every day is worse, and more, and more Nazis are around us.

He heard scattered murmurs and voices calling out, "Lord help us. Show us the way", and cried out, "We know. We know." We got to realize though that it may even get worse until we can make it better". He paused, and he said let us all pray". He spoke the words of prayer and the men all followed by repeating what he was saying, "Blessed be the Lord that we are still here and that we are able to do some good." They all said Amen.

The Priest continued speaking. His voice carried throughout the entire hall. The Americans are fighting all over Europe and will soon be here to free us from this horrible war and the frightening nightmare thoughts of continuous domination by the Nazis. I have reports that the Russians are fighting hard and winning against the Nazis." He paused, and it was evident that he was just about ready to cry for there were tears in his eyes, but he gripped himself and even gripped his right fist and continued speaking to the men and said, "Right now there are people hiding out in the woods that are good people. They are solid citizens of our Slovakian country. One thing I have to tell you is that they would help us if we were the ones in the woods". He cleared his throat, because it was becoming evident that he was having trouble voicing exactly what he wanted to say.

While the Priest continued his talk, all eyes of the men were glued to the Priest's face, and all ears were listening intently to what the Priest was saying. One could hear a pin drop. It was that quiet in the room with the exception for the Priest's talking. The light on the top of the candle flickered at the same time. He continued, "They, these people are literally starving. It is up to us to bring them food in spite of the snow and difficult winter weather conditions, and despite our understandable fear for safety for our families and ourselves". He continued, "We must help G-d and the angels do their job to help these people".

The Priest continued, "We all know that we can do it, and we will". He paused, and then said, "There are other priests out there that are doing the same thing that I am doing right now at this minute. Remember and remember well. You have only to fear G-d. You should never fear the Nazis. Man's fear of them has allowed them to conquer our country. We must say to ourselves that this is only temporary and that the Nazis are evil and that they should be destroyed."

He continued by saying, "Jon, my fellow Priest has come to me to ask us to organize men to go out into the woods and bring food to these people. He paused, and he asked, "Just for starters. While Jon and I still have a lot to do in organizing this journey, let us all start this journey of goodness by my asking, "Who would like to be in charge of gathering up bread and jam for these people?"

A hand went up quickly and the Priest said "Okay. Good".

Then the Priest said, "Who would like to gather all the cakes, and I mean one-hundred cakes"?

A voice from far in the back spoke loudly, and the man cleared his throat first, and said, "Yes, I will," as he stood up and faced the crowd.

I know that some of you are bringing food to some of these people as often as you can. That is good. That helps. That is beneficial to those people. Remember that when you help those people you help yourselves. We did not want the stench of murder, and blood, and pillaging on our consciences. We are good men. We are good Catholics. Above all, we are good Catholics. A lot of the men stood up and clapped. Some of the men whistled.

The Priest signaled the crowd to calm down by lowering his hands twice. The men took their places.

The Priest continued to talk, "We will need torches, maybe fifty torches. We will need at least 30 or say 40 sleighs. With the sleighs, we will need horses, at least one horse or two horses for each sleigh". He put his hand on his mouth as though thinking and then said, "Oh, maybe fifty horses or at least sixty or more horses. We will need plenty of food to put on the sleighs, oh, yes, plenty".

One man raised his hand. The Priest said, "Yes" and nodded his head and looked at the man. The man said, "I have five brothers that live close by. My brothers will help me to find the sleighs, and horses, and the torches, and our wives will bake the foods. The Priest started to smile as he said, "Yes. The more the merrier, yes that sounds good".

The next man raised his finger, and asked, "How will we hide all of the food from the German Nazis?" The Priest's answer was spontaneous. He said, "Hide it anywhere where you know the German Nazis will not find the food. Hide it in corners of your cellars. Hide it in clothes. Hide the food in hats, but hide all the food well and then bring it for what we are going to call our Christian Christmas delivery in the woods". The Priest asked, "Any other questions?"

One man raised his hand, "Looks like we only have one week to put this all together". The Priest answered with a smile on his face saying, "Yes. We only have one week, but we can do it." The other men looked on. The Priest walked amongst the men. He encouraged them by saying, "Bake an extra cake every day this week and you already have seven cakes". The farmer, and the tall man, and the short men nodded their heads in affirmation.

The man, Nicolas raised his hand a second time. All of the other men sat quietly. Some sat hunched on their chairs bearing witness to a hard few years when they had to plow the lands and plant all of the crops all by themselves. "Yes", the Priest motioned to Nicolas, "What was it that you wanted to ask?" "How are we going to organize such an enormous undertaking?" The Priest stood with his feet firmly placed on the podium, and he arched up his back. He called out to the crowd, "The Lord is with us. When we walk in the paths of righteousness, the Lord walks with us". He looked at the crowd and said, "If each of you does his part, we will be able to accomplish this task".

Another man raised his hand and said, "My wife always makes my favorite, which is cornbread," and he asked, "Is that okay?" The Priest responded quickly, "It is more than okay, but tell your wife to bake at least 70 of the cornbreads". The man responded, as he laughed and the crowd laughed softly with him, saying, "That means that we will have 70 corn breads in which to feed the poor, and the needy, and remember, he said, "These people are starving". The Priest then said, "Who else would like to share with us what they are going to bring?"

A third man raised his hand and the Priest motioned to him with his hand that he should speak. The man asked, "What happens if the weather is bad and we cannot deliver the food on that night before Christmas?" The Priest shook his head back and forth and then said in a tone of affirmation, "The weather will be good that night, but there is nothing to worry about, we could always deliver the food a day late". The Priest smiled and said, "You know I am betting that no one out there in the woods has a calendar". He smiled and said," No one knows what time it is either."

All of the men laughed. Some of the men looked a little tired for they were leaning their heads down. The Priest noticed this and said, "Okay, just another minute more. Jon and I will be coordinating everything, and Jon, and I will come to your farms and keep you informed on when we all meet, where we all meet, and when we all go into the woods".

A voice at the end of the last row asked, "Will we have some security on this mission?" The Priest said, "Yes. Undoubtedly we will need men with guns, and Jon, and I will be meeting tomorrow morning early to work out the plans for the security. Rest assured. You have nothing to fear. You are doing G-d's work and you will be all right, through the whole mission. This is just precautionary".

Another man raised his hand, but he was slow to ask his question. He asked, "What if the Nazis find out about this?" The Priest answered, "We are doing God's work by delivering food to the starving people out in the woods". The Priest gripped both of his hands and said, "Let the Nazis find out. They will never succeed in stopping us".

The Priest continued as he said, "Just one more thing. I know that the war has affected us all, but we also know that G-d has allowed us to live in our homes, and be with our families, and bake our breads and cakes". He said, "We must share breads and cakes with our friends and neighbors. G-d will reward us if we do".

One man raised his hand, and the Priest called on him. The man asked, "Should we share this information about all of this equipment with our wives?" The Priest answered back swiftly, "We are going to go into the woods in Micholovce with lighted torches. We are going to bring breads, and cookies, and milk, and eggs, and cakes to the people who are hiding in the woods and that is all that I know, but if you want my advice, tell no one except your wives and only speak with the people who are in this room". There was silence.

The man whose name was Don asked, "But how can we do this? It is such an enormous task?" The Priest answered, "It is God's will that we assist these people who are in dire need, and we shall do it", and his voice sounded very firm. There were no more questions from the men sitting in the group. There was only silence. The Priest said, "Jon and I will be talking to all of you very shortly. The Priest paused and breathed in heavily. The Priest said, "We have to remember that there are just seven days to organize all of this, but we can do it". He paused and still stood at the center of the podium so no one moved from their chair. No one would leave. They were all absorbed in the task of reaching out and extending their help to those who were really needy. All for the exception of the man who sat in the midst of all of them for his thoughts were rotating first, fast, and furious. He was panting and pacing inside of himself. He was designing a plan in his mind. He was going to wait for everyone to leave and then he was going to look for the main office for a radio. He was ready and waiting to tell the Nazis waiting for his call all that went on in the church. No one suspected him as a Nazi soldier. He smiled to everyone and sat with the others. No one suspected. No one asked him questions.

❊　❊　❊

The Nazi Looks For A Radio in the Church

The men and the women piled out of the church. It was dark outside. They all quickly disappeared. The Priest stood by the front door. He was watching the people going back to their homes. When the cloak of darkness covered all of the fading images of the people, he walked back into the church and went to where he had his room. He looked for his Bible, and he found the Bible on the top of the bureau. Just as he had reached for the Bible, he heard a voice, but he wasn't sure that it was a man's voice or the radio sending signals. The Priest had kept a radio hidden in his office. He sometimes received word of what was happening from the Partisans. He listened more carefully and he determined that someone was turning on the radio. He walked quickly out of his room and through the church prayer room and he headed to his office. He came just in time to see a man who had been in the crowd carrying the radio in his hands and fleeing from the church from one of the side doors. The Priest knew what to do. He ran to the steps of the bell tower and when he could reach the rope that rang the bells, he pulled hard and the bells rang. The Priest rang and rang the bells. The villagers who had left the church stopped straight in their tracks. They turned around and ran towards the church. One man yelled out, "It is the Priest calling us. Hurry back to the church", he cried. One man reached the church ahead of the others. He grabbed one of the front door's handles and he pulled the door open. The other men flooded into the church. The Priest yelled, "Run after that man. He stole the radio from the office. Hurry up and run after that man. The Priest pointed to the direction that the man had taken. Two men in the crowd left the church and headed towards the village. They were unnoticed by the others. Their destination was to go as far as possible away from the town.

One farmer yelled out to the others. Let us go in all directions. I will take ten men with me. Another man yelled for the crowd to follow him. There were others who went in groups of five to pursue the Nazi. The Nazi carried the radio under his left arm. He made haste for the cottage. He knew that no one would find him there. He thought to himself, "Suppose the hunter is in his cabin?" He made plans in his mind to dupe the hunter, and to kill him if he needed to. He was determined to get to the cabin. He was determined to send a message to his headquarters. It was pitch black outside. Except for the snow and ice that reflected the light, there was no light to show the way. The Nazi knew his way however and was heading straight for the cabin and would be there shortly. The men who were pursuing him could not find tracks in the darkness to follow him. It was slow going for the pursuers. They had not rested and were tired before they began the pursuit.

The three angels were parked for a rest high up above the mountains. The Nazi reached the cabin in record time. Not finding the hunter, he quickly went to work on the radio to make it send a relay message to his command. He kept pressing and turning the knobs on the radio. Then after an excruciating ten minutes and having no patience left, he turned the knobs completely from right to left. He heard voices. They were German voices. He turned the knob to send and announced who he was. There was silence at first. There was a lot of static then. The Nazi was intent, however, in sending the message. He announced himself again. The door to the cabin flew open. In walked the hunter. He aimed his rifle at the Nazi. The Nazi put his hands up. He said to the hunter, "I will give you passage to Germany. You will have a fine life in Germany". "Never you mind about a fine life, not where you are going", and he waved his rifle for the German to go to the open door. The German agreed, but just as quickly caught the top of a pistol that was hidden under his jacket and aimed it at the hunter's chest and released the trigger of the gun. The hunter staggered, but managed to get out one bullet. The bullet grazed the Nazi. The men who were coming up the mountain heard the rifle's shot and yelled, "This way. Come this way". The Nazi knew that he was being pursued. He reached for the radio. At that moment, the female angel sent a signal to the radio to disable it and it became hot to the touch. The Nazi soldier grabbed the radio, but could not hold onto it. He dropped it on the floor. He looked at his hands. The palms of his hands were red from the heat of the radio. He knew to run. He ran out the front door. The men were coming up the nearby hill and they spotted him. One man yelled out, "There he is. There he is. Get him". And the fortunes of war for these few moments were reversed. Numbers of good men and women were pursuing the lone bad guy. Fortunes were reversed. The angels from their cloud high up above were enjoying this scene. They were ready to help the good people in any way. They were waiting to see how the situation would develop. The Nazi ran and ran. The crowd came coming after him. He reached for his revolver and fired at the crowd. The bullets did not reach their mark. His aim was off and the bullets missed. Realizing that he had no bullets left, he threw the gun into the woods. The pain in his toe began to throb. He knew that he could not continue on this trek for long. He looked for a place of refuge. He saw the lake up ahead and ran for it, noticeably stumbling along the way. He jumped into the water and swam towards the middle of the lake. The crowd stopped once they saw where he was. They stood and they watched. The Nazi inched closer and closer to the center of the lake. He reached the center and then was swimming towards the shore of the lake on the far side. He was reaching for distance as he pulled and pushed the water away from himself. Reaching and panting, and kicking his feet harder and harder, he swam away to the distance of the shore. Waves splashed high into the air as his legs flapped and kicked at the water. Then there was a bang. He knew not to search in the direction of the sound. He knew to push, and to pull, and to kick the hardest that he could. He had almost reached the edge of the shore when the water would not let him push and pull. He could hardly keep himself above water as he twisted and turned in the water and flapped his hands on the top of the surface of the water. Underneath him rose a torrent of water that was flowing forcefully and becoming more and more forceful as each moment passed by. The waves from the bottom of the lake rose higher and higher until the waves forced their way high into the sky. A whirling pool of water formed higher and higher until its waves reached the sky. In the center of the whirlpool arose the wicked-looking head of a dragon. As the whirlpool rose higher and higher, the figure of the dragon emerged high up above the waves. The Nazi soldier began to feel frightened. He began to visualize himself as drowning in the water. He was frightened. The dragon moved his body above the water and flapped his 70 feet of tail back and forth in the water. The Nazi was losing all hope. The tail of the dragon whisked him up high above the water and the dragon's hand caught him in his grip. The dragon looked at him with his two bulging eyes as he moved his head to one side and then to the other. The dragon snarled and opened up his mouth. He was contemplating whether or not to eat the Nazi. He decided to throw the Nazi away into the whirlpool. The Nazi screamed from fear as he fell into the rotating whirlpool. Then just as suddenly as the whirlpool appeared, it slowed down and receded into the depths of the lake. The dragon followed and dived down deep for his home on the bottom of the lake. The water settled. All became calm. The town's people went back to their homes. They covered themselves up with quilts and blankets, and were warm, and safe in their beds, and in their homes. The Priest retired for the night, but said his prayers for the village people and for the poor, innocent souls who might or might not survive the cold weather of the night.

❄ ❄ ❄

The Next Day Arrived

The next day arrived as a vision for the future and as a welcome guest, as a visitor for the present. The crest of the bright, shining sun shined upon all who were righteous with outstretched hands of prayers. Blessings were bestowed on all who were good people.

Yet the war raged in the distance. Echoes of bangs and banging, and whistling, and whirling, and booms, and crying, and yelling---all the intrepid, tepid sounds of war---all sounding, and resounding, and echoing from the mountain tops of the cities and towns in Slovakia. The sounds passed from one mountain top to the other and filtered down from one ledge of the mountain to the other. Small flying objects infiltrated, and penetrated the air up above the trees, and all that nature and G-d has provided. Articles of fire, and ashes, and debris looked like insects flying all around in all scattered directions. Evidences of more deadly debris came and circled the targeted war area over and over again dulling and diming the sun's penetration from the sky.

At the same time as the deafening, defying sounds were heard, visual perceptions of real-life pictures of lighted visions of homes, and buildings, and trucks, and tanks on fire, of fireball bombs falling and falling and then crashing on their mark could be seen. The projection of the firebombs traveling its mechanical arc and landing near its mark or on its mark, visions of the peacefulness and brilliant colors of a rainbow were nowhere to be seen. These visions were on every person's mind. Everyone saw the stark raving, deadly realistic scenes. These sights could never be forgotten. These sights forged indelible prints into the ridges and caverns of the mind.

The sounds of the hissing of bombs as they flew through the air was resounding, and resounding, and it echoed through the trees, the mountain tops, and the mountain ridges, and through the mountain passes, onto an elongated track of its own. Throughout the chilling experience, and the defying of air, there could be heard the war sounds. One could only grip oneself with feelings of stark terror. The bad sounds echoed and re echoed in the ears of people over and over again. When one bomb died out or found its mark, another quickly took its place. The double, triple, quadruple staccato sounds of the war was chilling down to the bone and produced large goose bumps on the skin. As the bombs hit their targets, the thud of the sound was deafening from the force of the impact, forcing one to kneel down on his knees and pray for silence, and even beg for silence. Prayers echoed resistance to the horrors throughout the mountain tops of the mountains, and the ridges of the mountains, and through the embers and leaves of the trees, saying, almost screeching and screaming the words with all kinds of accents, "No more. No more. Please, dear G-d. No more." The angels were listening and they were doing their best.

Stories Told By Partisans As They Met
Joseph Or Anna Outside The Bunker

From the stories told by Partisans that somehow came to be told to the Freier family, Anna could vividly visualize the Nazis going from house to house in Micholovce while rounding up their victims. She had seen how the Nazis had come to her neighbor's houses. One always knew that the Nazis were coming. There would always be flares of sands flying in scattered directions along the tracks of the Nazi motorcycles. They would always send two messengers before the trucks arrived. The messengers rode on motorcycles and usually wore thick glasses on their goggles. When the sand started to churn and create the illusion of a sand storm, all people who were watching for the Nazis began to accept the reality that many of them would be taken away and would never come back.

The Nazis would drive up to a house with three or four trucks. They would surround the house and knock with vengeance and pound on the front doors with long rifles. If no one answered the front door, they would shoot through the windows and kick down the door. It was an instinct from within their mad psyches to sometimes pull out the pin from a grenade and throw it into one of the windows. They wanted to make sure that if they could not round up the Jews, then no one in the house would be allowed to survive. The Partisans and the Russian soldiers would see the smoke coming from the center, fronts, and backs of these houses, and the leaders would silently motion to them that they should go one, and then another, and go over there. The partisans always walked brusquely, but at a steady pace. They walked up mountain ridges that were covered with fresh snows. They would never stay long in one place. They were the nomads of the desert of the destruction of Slovakia by the Nazis. Their guns were carried in front of them always and at all times, and they walked with a steady step of putting one foot before the other, and they were ready to fire their weapons in an instant.

When they spotted the Nazi soldiers attempting to leave a house that was just gutted with smoke, they would fire upon them. The Nazis would get down on the ground and fire back. Gun fire would be exchanged for many fateful minutes. While the dead inside the house lay dormant, and unhearing, and no longer hopeful of reprieve from such madness. Sometimes the bullets did not find their marks. The partisan's marksmanship was expert, but their fingers were sore, and many times frozen so that even if their aim was steady, the fingers on their hands hesitated. Sometimes the bullets that the Nazi shot from their guns pierced through the bodies of the innocent partisans and also hit the persistent Russian soldiers. Sometimes, the bullets of the Partisans would find their mark and a Nazi would no longer be able to kill and maim. He too would lie still in the cold, and bitter ground, and the blood would ooze out of his now lifeless body. Any inch of goodness that was in his body did not have the chance to show. Any talents that he possessed did not have a chance to materialize and benefit others in a good way. Gone was his life for this madness of conquering and defeating all armies in Europe. It was shear madness, but they all followed. That was more the crime that was committed. It was a loss of good minds and purpose that would help society and benefit people for generations to generations that was the real loss. It was undeniably so the same loss on the side of the predators as for the side of the victims. Not every Nazi wanted to do evil and kill. The Nazis were commanded to commit evil by the man who was in charge and his name was Adolf Hitler. Adolf Hitler's name will forever go down in history as a barbarian tyrant. The other Nazis, the ones who followed his orders had a chance to do good and go down in history as persons who accomplished something worthwhile. The majority of the Nazis chose to follow and to do evil. It was their choice and the Nazis had to be stopped. If they could not be stopped and conquered by the Slovakian army, then they would have to be conquered and overcome by the American armies under the command of General Patton. The Nazis were to be overcome, history tells us, by also the Russian leaders. This was besides the American soldiers, who fought bravely to free the people in all over Europe from the Nazi bondage.

Many times winning the battles against the Germans was a matter of chance, but it was also a matter of determination to defeat the evil Nazis. The American generals knew that they had to defeat the Nazis at all costs. There was no other way out. Otherwise, the Nazis would become powerful enough to take over the United States.

Thus, this determination to free individual countries and all of Europe from evil leaders were the deciding factors. Intelligence played a large role in the defeat of the Nazis even though the Nazis claimed they were going to win the war no matter what happened. The Russians were skillful in camouflage. The Russians were battling to win back Moscow. This feat ultimately was the turning point of the war. The Germans were going to lose the war from that battle on. The German's poor intelligence of what was going to happen, and where, and how was one of the major reasons for the defeat of the Germans. The German intelligence history had proven only effective in detecting groups of pockets of resistance against them.

The help of the partisan soldiers was a major factor in winning the war against Germany. It was more than anything else a morale feature that there was a band of soldiers out there evading the German armies and fighting a guerilla warfare that could strike at any moment in time. The partisans evaded the bullets and gunfire from the Nazis as much as possible. When the right moment was ripe to strike, they used the trigger of their rifles, they pulled out a round that was unstoppable. The problem was that the Partisans and the Russian soldiers were outnumbered. They would have to retreat and so the Germans would win the battle and the war would go on. To be able to escape from the Nazis was also a victory. It was quite a victory and it meant that they would have other days to fight against the Nazis and try to defeat them once and for all.

The fighting had abated, but slowly abated. The hills and the mountain tops no longer shuddered from the encroachment of resounding echoes. The winds no longer carried the awful and unforgettable stench of the dead and the dying. The rivers flowed with white crests and occasional floating logs. The fish swam in swarms no longer shattered from uncontrollable tides and forces from the ripples of the sounds of the machine guns and tank barrages. Birds no longer shrieked through the air and no longer lost their feathers from fright of the sounds. The roots of the wild grasses halted their traumatized burrowing into the ground and instead they spread through the fibers of the earth and the wild grasses grew straight and tall and upright and basked in the rays of the shining sun.

The resurgent Slovak Army that had come back to their homeland from Britain after escaping to Britain when Hitler took over Czechoslovakia, tried to win back their country, but unfortunately capitulated to the forceful and dominating force of the Germans. Many of the Slovak soldiers escaped the hateful vengeance of the Nazis and joined partisan groups. They would continue to come down from the mountain to fight against the Nazis. They were, of course, trained soldiers in all types of warfare. They were without a doubt a reason for the survival of many of the partisan groups and the survival of many people hiding in the woods. They were an effective force in training men and women in military warfare and how to hide, and evade, and to defend themselves against the Nazis. They also were schooled in withdrawal techniques. Knowing they were around in the mountains and in the woods provided comfort for all those people who were hiding from the Nazis. The partisans were a symbol of hope to all those people who were hiding. The partisans were everyone's heroes. People knew that the Americans were there in Europe, but they did not see them there in Slovakia. There was only hope that the

Americans would come to free them. The Partisans were a reality until the Americans really did come to defeat and drive off the Germans from Slovakian and other country's soils.

Anna Looks for the Place Where the Battle Was Being Fought

The two of them, the mother and the son, Anna and her son, Martin, looked at the direction where they could see the smoke. They looked to find out where the battle was being fought. They thought of the people still left in the homes in Micholovce. They saw smoke coming from the direction of Micholovce and from the towns beyond Micholovce. Anna said the words out loud. "They are fighting in our town. It must be that the partisans have come to Micholovce". She sighed and held her son's hand. Martin shivered from the cold. Their noses were bright red and their lips had turned a slight purple color. But they knew in their hearts that they had a chance to survive.

Anna with Her Son, Martin, Outside the Bunker

Instead of telling Martin to go down to the shelter, she told him to stand tall, and she wrapped her long shawl around him. He leaned next to her body. And his body gave her some warmth. He was practically as tall as she was. She was a woman of small stature, but she had immense inner-strength. Anna redirected her son's thoughts. She knew it was best to tell him to watch the birds flying and to see the green colors of the leaves on the trees. She moved some of the locks of almost blond hair that was covering his ear, and she whispered, "Hold on. Tomorrow will be a better day".

He understood. He said quietly, "We need to be strong". They remained by the tree standing for a long time. It was as though they had become like the trees that they were standing next to. As trees, they stood tall and erect. As trees, they never flinched from the sounds of the battles. As trees, they knew that after winter, their leaves would become greener and shine more in the glow of the sun. They didn't speak for a long, long time. Minutes passed into hours. It was their silent moments to be together, and they both knew that it was most precious.

They realized at the same time that it would soon be dark. They knew that they had to look for food. Martin understood his mother's thoughts. He asked, "Could we scrape some of the bark from the pine tree with my small knife and then cut off some of the wood from the pine tree? Anna answered "yes". She helped him mold the knife into the fibers of the wood of the tree for he knew that Anna had done this last week when they could not find any food. She said, "If we boil these pieces of pine wood and chew on them well, we will have something to sustain us". Martin said, "Yes", and he was proud that he could help find the food. Before they left the tree, Anna picked off some of the pine needles. Martin knew that she was going to make some tea with the pine needles. He remembered what his father told him just minutes before he had gone out of the bunker this day. His father told him to pick some leaves from the beech tree, because the leaves were good to chew on. Martin reminded his mother. A beech tree was only a few feet away from where they were standing, and it was easy to gather the leaves. With pockets full of pine tree wood, and beech leaves, they walked proudly towards the bunker. As they entered the bunker, it was almost dark. They looked around the outside perimeter of the bunker, around the pine tree that they were standing around, and at the beech tree. They followed each other's glances and looked over to the lake. "I would like to have some grayling fish. I can sink my teeth into the meat of the fish. It tastes so good", Martin said, as he rolled his tongue. "Well, Anna said, "Sometimes there is a break in the winter and the weather gets warm. If you can be careful leaning into the lake, maybe, just maybe then you can find a fish". They both looked one more time at the outside. They longed to see a lone man walking through the woods. He would carry a nap sack on his back. They would know that he was not a Nazi. He would wear a brown cap. The cap was a plain dull color of brown, but inside there was a blue lining. They were sure any way that a Nazi would never come alone. They were right for the Nazis never traveled alone. The Nazis always came in packs. They were wolves disguised as men.

Anna poured the little bit of oil that she had left, put about a quart full of snow into her large wrought-iron pot and used one of the few matches that she had left to light a fire. She threw in some pieces and cooked the pine wood. The bits and pieces of wood cooked well and softened. As she stirred the pot, she thought to herself, "I would have loved to have had some potatoes to boil". She kissed the tips of her fingers. She started to think about the grayling fish. "What a beautiful fish it is, with its iridescent scales, and the soft palatable fish that was absolutely scrumptious". "OH", she remembered, "What a beautiful fish" and the meat on its bones so sweet and succulent". Joseph came up to her and said, "Thanks Anna for taking such good care of us". Sam said that they were waiting in anticipation for the food". He said that the other children were going to pretend that they were eating latkes". It was a happy moment. They all laughed. They savored the food and all ate it slowly and drank down the pine needle soup. It was nourishing. They were not going to starve. They were trying their best. They lay down and rested after their meal.

❄ ❄ ❄

The War Continued To Rage

Anna knew that the Americans had invaded parts of Europe. Even though they were alone in the bunker, they had known about this development in the war before they had escaped to the woods. She remembered the partisans who had come to visit with them about a month ago. The Partisans knew everything that was happening in Slovakia. They traveled constantly in fear of being caught by the Nazis. The Partisans knew where a lot of people were hiding and once in a while they would come for some food to some of the places they knew were safe. If they stayed for the night, it would only be until the sun set and the darkness of the night was gone. The Partisans always made sure that it was safe to leave a place in hiding, and they would cover their tracks better than anyone knew how. They used the pines from the pine tree to swish away any signs of their footprints. Sometimes they would walk in circles and then find their destination. They all were familiar with the woods, and the mountain, and this knowledge was their saving grace.

A Chilling Noise At Nighttime

Late at night there was a chilling noise. It was like the scratching of nails against the firm wall of the underground bunker. Sam was the first one to hear the noise. Anna who very rarely slept and when she did sleep, she slept with one eye open, did not hear the noise at first. The others slept soundly almost in their own world of dreams. Anna got up and Sam got up. Together they realized that the noise was coming from the room in the bunker that was in back of them. Sam walked into the room and looked around. It was dark inside the bunker most nights, and the room in the back was considerably darker. Sam tried to listen carefully to follow the sound of the scratching, rocking noise. In the first room, there was light that filtered down through crevices amongst the boughs of pines. On many nights, small night lights filtered light from the shine of the moon and the shining rays of the stars. Sam looked and looked and could not find at first where the noise was coming from. The animal must have seen him and stopped scratching for a time. He put aside thoughts of fears, and he moved deeper into the bunker room. Two shining lights grew to be evident once his eyes got used to the dark better. In a moment's time, he realized that he had spotted two small round, revolving eyes. The eyes were focused steadily on him. He looked for more details, because at this moment he had to know what he was dealing with. His eyes squinted and his lips firmed up, and then he realized what he was dealing with. He saw a nose and two large ears and he knew what he was dealing with. Sam called to Anna, who was waiting anxiously on the side of the entranceway and announced, "It is a rat". Anna said to Sam, "We may not be able to find food for tomorrow. See if you can catch the rat. Sam reached with his hand and tried to smack a hard smack at the rat. He told Anna, "All I need is for the rat to stand still in a moment". The rat looked scared and tried to climb up, but Sam's hand was aimed at the fleeting animal. It was a contest of who was fastest. The rat was running at a very quick speed. It was going higher and higher until it reached the ceiling of the cave room. Sam could not catch the rat. He ran deeper into the cave, but the rat's eyes were on Sam. Sam called out, Bernard, come in here quickly. Anna quickly left the room. She held both hands on the cheeks of her face. She blew hard into the air and walked quickly to the edge of the first room. Joseph called out to her, "Anna, calm yourself down. It is only a rat." He tried not to laugh, but after a few seconds, he muttered the words, "Hee, Hee," and Anna relaxed and she came up to him, and she sat down on the chair that Joseph and the boys had made for her. Anna said to him, "Joseph, what will be?" Joseph said to her in a calm voice, "Anna we made it this far, and we are going to survive." She looked at him and laughed too. Joseph said to her, "You see if the rat had not come, you would not have laughed. Anna said to him, "Joseph, help the boys to catch the rat and maybe you can fix the rat up so that we can eat it". Joseph looked at her with the expression on his face as if to say, "This war and what it brings us to do", but did not speak the words out loud for he knew that Anna would cry. Joseph held his hands out to Anna. She rose from her chair. Her rose from his chair. They embraced. No kissing. They held each other tightly and they both did not want to let go. Anna coughed a little. Joseph let her go. Joseph said to her, "Another day will come. We will all dine well". Tears streamed from Anna's eyes. Edith went to her mother. She rubbed her mother's shoulder.

During the Nighttime While Anna and Her Family Were Asleep

Coming up over one of the ridges a few miles away where Anna and her family were hiding was a lone man. He wore a distinguishable brown colored cap on his head. He was a tall man and even thought of as a giant, but he was very lanky so he had no trouble fitting into any crowd of people. He could easily slip out of any crowd of people. His grandmother had once been a Jew. He remembered his grandmother. She was a good woman. A man that he had known for a long, long time had come to see him a few days ago and asked for his help to bring food to the man who had before been his boss. The two men saw each other in church a lot, and he agreed to bring food to Joseph, Anna and her family.

The man had put on his jacket and put on his brown cap. The coffee and the buns that he had just eaten were kind of swishing in his stomach, but he knew that tonight was the best time to deliver the food to Anna and her family. He too had known the family and he liked them. He said to himself, "Not bad out. Not too cold, and it does not look like it is going to snow."

He made steady strides through the snow, giving the impression that he traveled alone and did not wish to follow or lead anyone else as he fit through the spaces between the trees in the woods. From the look of the steady steps, one could easily determine that he was on his own and that he was determined to complete his mission. His strides were long. His gait was steady. He had a knapsack concealed under the back part of his jacket. It was not a very large knapsack, but it nevertheless concealed two loaves of rye bread, and three dozen sugar cookies with nuts on the top of each cookie; and the rest of the knapsack was filled with chunks of fresh chocolate bars and dried apricots. The man muttered to himself as he continued his steady stride, "I promised the foreman that I would bring these people food. I should reach them by night fall. I shall look for the clearing in the front of the pine trees and for the pine that has had its lower branches cut away. If no one is outside their bunker, I am to leave the knapsack on the ground near the pine trees after I cover it up with as many pine boughs that I can find.

He stopped for a moment, but it was not because he had to catch his breath. He knew these woods backwards and forwards for as a young boy he had always gone hiking and hunting with his cousins and father and his uncle. He recalled to himself sadly," my uncle and two of my cousins are gone now. They died too soon. This war is awful." He shook his head, looked all around him for any signs of lights or movements. When there were none that he could see or hear, he picked up his pace. He continued until he spotted the pine trees. He had an expression of relief on his face even though his face looked ruddy and weather worn. The soreness on his face did not seem to bother him. He knew that he had to do his part to make this world a better one. He had to do his part to counter the Nazis and their wrongdoings. He had to free himself from guilt over what people were doing to people. He shook his head in disgust. It was dark out and there was no one outside the bunker. He knew not to knock on the bunker, but as he said to himself, "In this darkness, I may step onto a trap and then where would I be? I must make it home by early morning to my wife and two daughters". Bending down low just to be safe that no one saw him, he took his jacket off quickly and pulled the shoulder straps of the purple-colored square shaped knap sack off of his shoulders. Putting his jacket back on, he positioned the knapsack of food and then with a haste that is not often seen, reached with a strong grip and tore off branches from a pine tree and covered up the knapsack. He looked back at the path that he had come from. He would follow his footsteps quickly, but he would take some of the pine branches and cover up his tracks as he descended down the mountain pass. He walked quickly as though the edge of the burst of lightning would catch him and that was something that he did not want. While he walked, he reached for the small pistol that he carried under the belt of his pants. He just wanted to make certain that he had the pistol if he needed to use it. He walked briskly and steadily down the mountain pass towards the town of Micholovce. The night light from the moon and the stars guided him on his path. The trees that he passed grew in clusters, and he knew that if he stayed clear of the clusters that the light would help to guide him. He was confident that he would make it back safely, but walked briskly all the way without stopping. When he reached the town, he did not go directly to his house. He walked within the edge of the forest and then doubled back. It was almost sunrise when he knocked seven times quietly on the back door. He wife tapped back 7 times quietly and then he knocked one more time. She opened the door. She hugged him. "You see you did some good", but she sighed, "I was very worried". He cleared his throat and walked into the warmth of their cottage-type small home, and said, "You are right to help those that are in dire need. The Nazis will win this war otherwise, and we do care that those rats lose the war". She said, "Come on into the kitchen, and I will make you a cup of hot tea". She walked quickly, and he followed her and kept in step and said, "Hey give me some of those sugar cookies. Give me the ones with the walnuts on the top". She smiled and said, "Yes. "I will put the cookies on a plate. The pot of hot water had been whistling for a while on the stove". The smoke from the pot cleared his nostrils, and he relaxed, sat back in the wooden kitchen-style chair, and he bit into some of the cookies". "Hum, these are really chewy", he said as he looked at the contours on his wife's body. He said, to himself, "She is a very beautiful woman and a good one too".

❀ ❀ ❀

On the Fourth Day of Waiting For The Food Delivery Before Christmastime

It was the fourth day of waiting for the man who was hired to bring the food. Anna had climbed up the ladder one rung at a time, counting the twelve steps and feeling a little dizzy when she came to the top step of the ladder. She had come out by herself again once more. She really did not wish to leave the bunker, but she knew in her heart that she had to be vigilant. She had to see and hear what was going on around her and her family. There was no other way to know what was happening. Joseph had wanted her to stay inside the bunker. He said to her, "The man will come and we will most likely hear his footsteps. She was not assured, but did not want to upset her husband.

She asked herself the question, "What will be?" She could not answer. She could not cry. "Life is for the moment and one must take advantage of each of these moments", she whispered to herself. She looked up into the sky as she cleared the entrance hole of the bunker. She really looked a lot at the sky. She could see blueness that reached far beyond the eyes to the left and far beyond the eyes up high in the sky. The sky was a blue azure shade of color on this day and there were a few lines of pink dispersed carefully at the bottom of the sky, and the azure blue color of the sky was dotted with puffy white clouds, and the edges of the clouds that she saw, she looked very closely at that were almost faded gray. She muttered to herself, "Funny day today. But in spite of all the fine lines of gray color around the clouds, she saw a glimpse of a yellow circle. "Yes", she said to herself. Today will be a better day. I can feel it". She called to the sky, while holding her hands to the sides of her facial cheeks, "Send some of those yellow rays on me", and she shed a tear in her left eye. She reached up and beseeched G-d, as she said, "G-d I need you now. Please come down from your home in the sky and help me," she prayed. She wiped away the salt-water tear from the side of her face with a ruffled, muffled torn rag that had once been a clear, clean cotton fabric and very beautifully embroidered handkerchief.

She muttered to herself, "I have just been given faith that today will be a better day. Just maybe, maybe I can find some food. She walked out to the clearing of the pine trees. She remembered her dream the other day and she smiled, thinking what a warm-hearted experience". I should have told Joseph about my dream. He would have laughed and laughed. Then she stopped herself. She had heard a crackle-type noise. She asked herself the question, "should I look and look to see where the sound is coming from?" But she knew the answer. She had to look. She had the responsibility to investigate every sound, every odor, and any sight that was peculiar. After all, her family was with her. She cried for a few minutes and then looked out up at the sky. "Now to look for some food and to wait for the man who is to bring us some food." She was about to walk over to the beech trees, when in the corner of her eyes, she saw something gray move swiftly in the front of her. She said to herself, "Better tear off a branch from the pine tree. I need to defend myself". She quickly walked back to the pine trees. She was quick-witted. She was making a plan of defense for herself. She knew not to run back into the bunker. She knew to run away from whatever it was, and she was ready. From behind one of the pine trees, she was concealed. She waited and she listened and she watched. There was another crackling noise. She heard it. She saw it. It was large, and gray, and had a very large fluffy tail. It ran over to the clearing where there was a small bush. "Funny" she said to herself, "I did not see that bush before". Then she asked herself the question, "Why would the squirrel run directly to this bush?" She saw that the squirrel was sniffing at the bush and then she smiled for she knew that the man had come. "My G-d", she said to herself, "There is food under that bush," and she ran to the bush with all haste. She pushed away the many pine branches that the man had placed on the knapsack, and as she did she spotted a glimpse of some of the purple color from the knapsack. She looked up to the sky, and she cried, and she cried until she stopped herself. She pulled with the might of a good angel and the knapsack was released from its hold over the cotton material encrusted to the cold ground. "Oh, my", she exclaimed. "This is wonderful. I must bring this food to the children and to Joseph".

She looked all around the area to see if anyone had seen her find the knapsack and when she was sure that no one had seen her, she knocked on the bunker door the five taps and then the six taps and the door opened up and there was Sam. "Mom, come into the bunker", he said. He helped her to place her feet on the rungs of the ladder and down he climbed the twelve rungs and then down she climbed the twelve rungs. "Here", she said, "Here is the food". She opened up the knapsack and she reached in and pulled out a handful of cookies. It was a lightning effect. The word cookies naturally attracted attention, but when she showed the cookies to the family, each and every one of them got up from their stations and came towards her. She loved to see this. It made her think that there was hope. For a brief moment or two she forgot about the war. She grabbed a cookie for herself, and reminded her children and Joseph that there was also bread in the knapsack, as she said, "Eat, eat the bread first, and she took the bread out of the knapsack and tore off pieces and handed them out to the many hands that were extended and reaching out. Edith exclaimed first before all of the others, "This bread is so good. My, oh my".

Some Reminisces About Their Trek To Hide In The Woods

The Freier family fled into the woods to escape the Nazis. which bordered the main entrances of the town. Their luck was that they lived in Micholovce; Slovakia was one of the few towns that bordered the Russian borders. In order to escape the onslaught of the German army, its fierceness, and lack of regard for life, they had to move quickly to escape. The Russian borders had fewer guards, but further deep into their territory, there was a lot of security. The borders were always manned and without notice. The Germans did not come to Micholovce to 'collect' the Jews as they had come to other towns in Slovakia, because they needed large forces of German soldiers when they came to towns in Slovakia that bordered the Russian borders. The German commandants were always afraid of losing to the Russians.

They ran from their home almost naked. The Freiers ran from the Germans when they knew that the Germans were coming with a full force. They were wearing only their summer clothes—hardly clothed and chilled by the cold of the long, cold summer nights. When they heard gunshots in the background, and tanks firing their fierce rounds of ammunition, they got down on their knees and prayed for their lives. Joseph told his wife Anna, "We must all crawl through the woods. We have no choice but to crawl and hope for the best". They did manage to escape the fiercest onslaught that had ever come to the people of the town of Micholovce. When the family stopped for the first time in the woods, they realized that they had stumbled upon an oasis. Small quince trees, ripe with fruit dotted the landscap, and they were near a lake. The family fished for the grayling fish, and they ate the fish, and they were sustained. Weeks later they were found by Joseph's trusted foreman and a friend that both men trusted. They were brought food and clothing, which they warmly welcomed and were grateful for. They continued with this type of routine—fishing for the grayling, and eating the food that was delivered, and eating from the forest's bounty, until the winter of 1944, which was the coldest and the fiercest ever. The snow continued to fall for days. The temperature was icy cold and everything outside up above their underground bunker was frozen solid.

❆　❆　❆

On The Night Before Christmas

On the night before Christmas of 1944, Anna, climbed the ladder out of her bunker. The ladder was rooted well in the ground. The ladder was slanted. It was posted towards the sky. Unknown to Anna, the same three angels came down the ladder after she climbed up. The angels looked around the bunker. They saw the four sons and the one daughter. They saw Anna's husband. They climbed back up the ladder. While thinking over the situation, they flew back up to their cloud.

Anna knew that it was dark outside. She knew that it was probably pitch black outside so she would not be able to see much through the spaces of the trees. But she also knew that the ground was covered with snow which had patches of ice. Somehow the ice glowed and with the whiteness of the snow, there was light enough to see where she was going outside. Thoughts muddled quickly into her mind that night even as she was climbing out of the bunker and she felt instantly better about her situation when the cold air helped her to breathe better. Her thoughts, as always were what was going to happen to her and to her family? What was going to happen to them? What was going to happen to her children? Her thoughts converged quickly together about the war and the fact that she had made it---she and her family had survived the war up until now. Her thoughts got faster and faster. They got faster and faster until she had to stop at a standstill at the top of the ladder, and she felt her heart beat pulsating. Joseph was looking up from the bunker and wondered how his wife was. He called to her: "Anna, are you all right?" She did not look at him as she answered. She did not want to see that she was panting for breath and that she was crying. She answered quickly, "yes" to him and stepped out onto the ground. It was the middle of the night. She hardly knew the difference between day and night. The morning's rise of the sun, though, brought brightness to her hope. She knew that she was seeing the rise of another day. She had hope that her family would live another day.

❀   ❀   ❀

Anna Came Out Into the Wilderness To Pray For Her Family

She came to pray. She knew what to say. She had thought about what she would say. Every time that she prayed it seemed to be a little different. Her words were different. Sometimes she spoke to G-d about her children. Sometimes she spoke to G-d about her husband. Sometimes she told G-d that she was going to die soon from hunger. Sometimes she beseeched G-d and all of his powers. Sometimes she asked G-d to send down the angels to help them. Many times she told G-d that she could not go on. She would cry it out and then look up at the sky. She realized that she could not disappoint G-d. She knew that G-d knew about her peril. It was always her finest hour when she spoke to G-d for she knew that G-d would not forsake her. She said, "This prayer should be special. She thought to herself, "Maybe if I got down on my knees, it would make a difference, and she would have, but she knew that G-d would not forsake her. She had faith in G-d". In the black pitch color of the night, she came to say a prayer for the memory of her father and her mother. She recited the Kadish. She remembered her father. She repeated his name, "David

Hellinger". Her father had lived with the family. When his wife died, Joseph did not want David to be alone. David grew to enjoy the children. She remembered that Martin came to tell her a story about his grandfather. "Oh my", she said as she smiled and shook her head. The other children were playing outside, but Martin had a cold. Ana remembered that she told him to stay inside the house so that he could get better. Martin stayed in the house and drank a lot of tea and apple juice. He ate pieces of bread that were covered with apply cinnamon jelly. He read books about philosophers and tried to catch up on his school homework. He felt lonely. He knew that his grandfather had a room off of the kitchen. A large pantry had been made into his room. His grandfather loved the room. His grandfather always told him that he was where the action was and could always speak with someone in the kitchen or with someone in the house. Martin came down to his grandfather's room. He said, Grandpa, "I miss riding with you to deliver seltzer bottles to the people and their homes". His Grandpa laughed and said, "Yes. We had some good old times". Martin asked, "Grandpa. Could you walk with me to the window and help me to watch the children playing". "Sure", he answered, "and you know what I have a shawl that you can wrap around yourself so that you can pretend you are playing outside with your friends".

Anna Prayed For Her Children

She remembered to pray to G-d to save her five children, and her husband, and herself, who were literally starving to death. She stood there in the middle of the pitch-black dark night in no-man's land—deep in the heart of the woods that few people had ever seen. The chill dulled her thoughts. She was no longer afraid of dying; she stood there, almost rigid---in tattered and torn clothing, and in boots that no longer fit her feet---they had become so cold. She prayed to G-d to save her family for as she expressed with all of her strength that she had left, "they were innocent and deserved to live. At that moment, she remembered the many times that she had herself visited the Christian poor and had brought them wood to heat their stoves and their chimneys. The winter's weather had been so severe that they were unable to find food in the forest.

The Christians Celebrate Christmas

The Priest gave his speech at the church services on the night before Christmas Day. He spoke of Christ and his extension and goodness to all people. He spoke of Christ on the cross. The people sang hymns from the Bible. They all prayed together. There was togetherness amongst them. They reached out to one another. These were the people of the village. There were no strangers amongst them. They sang songs of peace, and tranquility, and of the baby Christ. It was a later service than usual, but no one thought anything about the time. At the end of the services, they all went down to the lower level of the church where there were baked apple pies, and lemon cakes, and lemon cookies, and there were spiced hams, and baked chickens, and there were bread puddings, and there were rice puddings, and there was a sumptuous chocolate cake with rich confectionary sugar icing. The Priest invited everyone to come join him for some festive food in the social hall.

It was an hour later and everyone had eaten and had drunk some of the teas and punch that were set out on the table. It was as though the clock had struck one and everyone turned into tin soldiers. Men whispered to each other. One by one the men left their families and left the church. Everyone seemed to go with the flow of the quiet action. They all knew what was going on. They acted as though nothing was about to happen. They acted as though this day was an ordinary day. One man whispered in the ear of another man at the table at the far end of the room. He said, "They found a sleigh for you". The other man listened intently and then nodded his head and winked his right eye in a sign of assent and as a sign of assurance that he would follow him.

These men and women walked out quickly disappearing quickly into the darkness of the night, but they could see each other. They knew what direction they were going in. None of them were trained soldiers, but they knew how to follow directions. They were most willing to do whatever was necessary to help those people who were starving in the woods. It was a group mentality that fosters love and caring. It was the Christmas spirit of giving and joy. These farmers knew the reality, because they had seen it happen during the war over and over again. They knew that the Germans were vulgar and bad. They knew that at any time the Germans could turn on them and collect some of them. They had seen it happen time and time again. They knew that as long as the Germans were in power that no one, absolutely no one was safe.

News of assassination attempts against Hitler trickled into their town. They knew that Hitler was the devil himself and that he had escaped with his life time and time. They knew that the war was long and it was costly in lives. They knew that the fighting for power triggered more fighting and more fighting. They knew that their own wives were in danger of being raped. They knew that the Nazis were drafting young boys from families from the towns to fight in the front lines and to defend their towns in Germany. They knew that at any time that the Nazis could come to shoot them on the spot. They remembered how it was before the war. They remembered the peace and tranquility before the Nazis came into power. They wished for the return of the peace and the tranquility.

The night air was brisk, but it was not a really cold night. The sky was dotted with shining stars. One of the men remarked, "It is a good night to go out and ride the sleighs in the woods". The other man nodded his head to say, "Yes". Everyone seemed to disappear into the night's darkness when they left the church. One could hear the church bells ringing in the distance. An hour later, men from all over the town converged on the front driveway of the church. Some of the men had arrived in a sleigh that was driven by one horse. Some of the men rode in sleighs that were driven by two horses. Some of the men rode horses. Some of the men drove wagons and the sleighs were piled up on the wagons. Other men drove wagons that were laden with packages of foods that had been prepared by all of the people in the town. It was to be a Christmas of goodness and mirth. It was to be a shining example of what good men could do in a war that was brutal, took tolls of innocent lives, and programmed German soldiers to become wanton killers with no sense of remorse.

The Hearing of Voices In The Wilderness

Anna climbed the steps of the ladder to the opening of the bunker. She was stifled with the inertia. She was stifled by her inability to take matters into her own hands. She was frustrated by not knowing what the next day would bring. She did not know if they would live or die. She did not know if the Nazis would discover where they were hiding. She poured out her feelings to G-d saying, "Favor me oh Lord and I will move mountains". She paused for a moment. It was a moment that seemed like an eternity. Out in the blackness of the night, she prayed that help would come. "Oh, Lord", she called out, send me a Moses. Send me a Moses. My people need to be delivered from this bondage". She remembered. She remembered reading about the Pharaoh in Egypt who refused to let G-d's people go. Moses came out of the desert. Moses returned to Egypt. He presented himself to the Pharaoh who had forsaken him and left him to die in the desert. Moses came time after time and told Pharaoh that he comes with the words of G-d and that Pharaoh must let G-d's people go out from bondage from Egypt. The Pharaoh at first promised to let the people go, but then reneged on his promise. At last Pharaoh gave in and said to Moses, "Go with your people out of the land of Egypt. Pharaoh reneged again. This time G-d saved the lives of the Israelites' first born sons, but took the life of Pharaoh's first born son and the lives of the first born Egyptian sons throughout the land. Pharaoh hastened to summon his generals, and he commanded them to follow the Israelites, and overtake them. Moses and the people had wandered through the desert and had come to the Red Sea. The people panicked. They could see clouds of dust from the approaching Egyptians in the far distance. The people beseeched Moses to help them. Moses raised his staff and the winds from the sky blew open a pathway through the sea. Moses and his twelve tribes of people walked through the pathway that G-d had allowed Moses to make through the sea. The people finished their journey along the pathway of the sea and the winds held up the waters from filling in the pathway. The people came to the other side of the shore, and they blessed G-d for saving them. They could see, however, the hooves of the approaching horses. They could hear the thunderous sound of the hooves hitting the sands of times and distances. The people could see the smoke rising in the air from the thunderous impact and crushing compacting on the pebbles of the sands. They could see and smell the dust in the air. The dust in the air blew with the winds. It was like waves from the ocean winding and swirling and moving rapidly with the force of the winds. They could only think that they had been forsaken and panic that the massive army that Pharaoh had commanded would overwhelm and overtake the Hebrew people. Moses raised his cane over the waters of the sea. Wild, ranting, dissident waves floundered over the pathway that had been made on the sea. The wild winds encompassed the Egyptian soldiers and threw them off of their horses and into the sea. The soldiers raced away from the winds as fast as they could, but they were no match for the strength of the swirling winds. The horses whinnied out of fear and raised their legs high into the air. It was all to no avail. The soldiers and their horses were swallowed up by the waves and the waters of the sea. Pharaoh sat mounted on his horse at the edge of the sea. He watched all of his army being swallowed up by the sea. He pulled and tugged at the reins of the magnificent stallion that he was riding. He rode all the way home to his castle. He knew that he had been punished by G-d for his cruelty against the Hebrews. He was still hardened. He would not repent.

Anna Hears Voices In The Wilderness

At the same moment that she ended saying her prayers, she heard voices—they were the voices of men and women. "Yes", she said to herself, "these are the voices from people who are outside in the chill of the cold and out in the darkness in the wilderness". "Yes. She said to herself, "This was the sound of people traveling through the woods in the darkness of the night and they were all singing." She could not imagine what was happening.

At that moment, she admitted to herself that she didn't even care if they were Nazi soldiers. She knew that she had a weak moment, but she was so hungry. The hunger was so difficult to bear. Her husband and her children were starving. She and her family had to have food. This was the biggest problem and the overtaxing and overwhelming concern. The bitter cold was bad enough. The fear of being caught by the Nazis was monumental. The fear of dying from hunger was an everyday reality. Hunger was her worst fear.

She looked in the direction where the sound of the singing was coming from. Pressure rose in her arms and extended to the tips of her fingers. She moved from foot to foot. Blood rushed to the top of her head. Her face turned red. Her eyes protruded. She could hardly find the inner strength to call out, but she knew that she must.

She saw sleighs moving in the distance, but not that far away, and she started to momentarily and without thinking any thoughts about it, to count them. She realized that there were many sleighs. The movement of the sleighs along the ice created a shining light of its own, and a sound of continuous motion along its own tracks, and she could see the images of the sleighs as they came up the hills in the forest and traveled through the spaces amongst the very tall and older trees. The sleighs were all driven by men who held the reins to horses; they came closer and closer. She saw lights from the fires from the lighted torches glowing in the night and providing light for everyone to see the forests. The fires on the tops of the torches lighted the way for the horses to pull the sleighs through the trees and through the distances that they knew or assumed that people were hiding.

In that very stark moment of reality, and life, and death decision to call out, and to signal to the sleigh drivers that she was here and in this spot and that she needed help, her mind wandered for a second. She thought of the story of the Macabees at Channukah time. They were an army of men who were greatly outnumbered by the invading Greek soldiers, yet they stood their ground, and they regained their strength, and fought on and won a victory for the Jewish people. Without her reaching out and calling out to the men who were driving the sleigh, the sleigh drivers might pass her by.

The sleigh drivers knew that there must be several people hiding in bunkers under the ground nearby to the lake. In those few minutes that she called out and the sleigh drivers did not hear her, Anna gripped herself saying, "What if I am wrong and it is a trick?" "No. no. no", she cried out. She cried out to G-d. "Help me and help my family". She was starving and her children were starving, and her husband was starving. She knew that there may never be a tomorrow. She had to take the chance. She knew that she had to take the chance. She would be devastated if they were bringing food to people in the woods and she did not get any of the food for her family.

She called out to these people with all of her strength and a shrill voice saying, "I am here. I am here". At first the muffled sounds of her voice were muted by the steady traction of the sleighs and the steady beat, beat sounds of the horse's hoofs. She called again and again until she could no longer mutter the three words that had so much impact. "I am here". She perched her lips and thought that maybe if I ventured out further into the woods, then they would see me. She was about to take one step forward when she saw a horse's face drawn in her direction. The horse saw her and the horse whinnied, and the horse's driver realized that the horse must have seen someone in the darkness of the night, and he looked out in the same direction and saw her.

He called out to the others, "Over here. Over here". She breathed in the cold air and blew it out, and she calmed down at that moment. She knew that they heard her cries for help. While waiting and while watching the three men come towards her, it was to her a signal of an eternity of time.

In that moment when she knew that they were coming to bring her food, she knew that she and her family would be saved. She recited a short prayer for an eternity of time to live and a requiem for those who had died unsaved.

She watched carefully as the three men came closer to her. She could make out their facial features now. They were ordinary people. They looked like farmers from the area. She watched as one man walked over to her, and then another, and then another. One of the men called out, "Here is one. Here she is. Come. Bring some food. Help her." He had the expression of being stunned when he walked over to her. Anna could understand his feelings of amazement. She knew what he was thinking. He was thinking that this was an unbelievable, incredible moment. She knew that he was asking himself the question, "how was it possible to find a woman standing out in the cold and in the darkness of the night? He was thinking what she was thinking that it was a miracle.

As he reached her, he exclaimed, "This is a Christmas miracle." She smiled and she said, "Yes". The second man to reach her brought her a blanket. He wrapped it around her and pressed it down on her back. She shivered for a moment with the blanket on, but then the warmth in her body returned. She had not realized that her body was that cold from the cold, raw weather outside.

The man asked her very politely as the two other men looked on, "How many of you are there?" She at first tried to voice her words, but couldn't. She looked at the men with good eye contact and there was an understanding expression in her facial expression. The men understood. They knew that she was afraid to answer the question. She breathed out and then caught her composure as she stepped a few steps backwards. She said in a voice that signaled strength beyond the ages, "Have you come to bring us food?"

The first man answered as he looked at her with kindness in his eyes?" "Yes. We have come to bring food to people who are hiding out in the woods." Her eyes were wide open and protruding in amazement. She could not speak any more. "Here, here are some cakes and some breads, and there are different kinds of jams. Here is a roasted turkey". He asked her if he could carry the food to the place where she was hiding.

She cleared her throat and with a profusion of tears, as she answered, "I will call to them and they will come to take the food". One man asked, "Would you like some wine?" She exclaimed, "Yes" with the voice of excitement. Another man brought five bottles of wine. Then one man said, "We have come from the church in town. The Priest has sent us to bring food to the hungry and the dying on this Christmas evening." Anna's eyes were still tearing, but she regained her composure and she said, "Someday we shall thank you". The man dropped his box full of cakes and breads on the white ground. He said, "Someday soon this wanton war will end. We shall dance yet in our homes to the merriment of Christmas time next year". Anna smiled and wiped away her tears and exclaimed, "Thank you for doing the work of the angels". And she proclaimed, "I would like that. I would like to celebrate Christmas with you and my family". The three men said, "Amen", and they said, "We will have to go bring some more food to people who are needy". They walked away to the glitter and the glow of the sleighs, which were laden with foods for the needy.

Anna waited for the sleighs to leave. She knew that she still had to be cautious. Joseph had always taught her to remember that the Nazis may be out there. Ana walked proudly to the opening of the bunker and she knocked.

The hatch opened and Sam called out to his mother, saying, Mom, "what has just happened?"

"Come", she said. "They brought us and the family food to eat for the Christmas and the New Year, and they announced the New Year that is coming. Anna came down the rungs of the ladder. Sam climbed up and Bernard was behind them. The two boys carried the three large baskets of food. Anna had taken off her coat and her hat. She was sitting in her chair. Joseph was standing by her side. Martin was waiting at the bottom of the ladder. Henry was drawing with a stick in the sand on the floor of the bunker. Edith was fitting twigs together to make a house out of twigs. Edith looked up as soon as the boys came down the ladder. Sam went down backwards while he pulled the basket down after him. Bernard threw down his basket to the ground and then climbed down. Sam ran up the ladder once again and carried the large basket frontwards as he nimbly placed his feet down the ladder rung. Martin stood quietly at the edge of the ladder ready to help Sam if he fell. The baskets of food were placed side by side. Together they filled up a large part of their small-quarters living room. No one ran to grab food. Everyone just breathed in and out and looked at the baskets. The baskets of food were indeed a miracle. Anna reminded Martin to run up the ladder and to close the hatch of the bunker. Martin climbed up and pulled at the rope from the inside of the hatch and the hatch came down.

Eating The Food That Was Delivered for Christmas

They were safe in the bunker. Now they had food. Anna said, "Let us all have some of the cakes". She passed out the small cakes and every one of them savored the food. Joseph said, "Before we eat, let us say a blessing for the cakes. They all said a prayer, which echoed throughout the bunker walls. The cakes were Christmas cakes. They were made with honey and a lot of dried fruits and nuts. Anna could see the pink color returning to the cheeks of her children. Anna smiled as she chewed the cake. Anna exclaimed, "There is wine for all of us to drink". Sam said, "I will go to the other room and get the cups". Joseph proclaimed, "Let us say a blessing". They all said a blessing. Joseph proclaimed, "Let us move the chairs and move the little table at the far right of the room". He muttered, "Anna take out some more food and let us all dine on a meal". She cautioned him, "Joseph, I will bring a little bit of food over to the table for all of us, but we must save some of this food". "Anna, you are right", he said, "But let us see what foods are in the baskets. They all came over to the baskets. It was the first time in weeks that the children seemed interested and curious in something. Anna had worked with them to continue to keep busy. Joseph had helped too. He was starting to lose hope though. Anna could see that. She knew that if she gave into any sense of despair that it would be the end of them. They would slowly lose hope and then they would give up. Anna wanted her children to live. She knew from the reports that she had heard from men that were delivering food to them that the war had to end soon. The family was told that the Russians were moving forward against the Nazis. They were told that the Americans were moving forward to counter the Nazis. She sighed as she looked at the food and breathed in heavily and said, "Looks almost like a mirage or a painted picture". She looked at the basket and counted all of the food in the basket. Joseph and the children were amazed. Sam wanted to grab some of the meat. Anna cautioned him, "The war is not yet over. We must conserve as much of the food that we can". She signaled with her hand for him to come over. She said, "Take a big piece of the meat". He smiled and pulled off a leg of the turkey. He smiled and smacked his lips. Joseph cautioned him, "Eat the turkey slowly". Next Anna said to Joseph, "Go bring some of the wooden forks and the wooden plates that we made. Joseph was back into the front room in a second. His legs seemed to have recovered from their feelings of ache and inertia. Anna smiled as she saw that the expression and the color in his face had improved. "Here", she said," as she passed out the plates, I will tear off some of the pieces of the turkey and will pass the meat to you". Each one of the children found a place to sit and chewed the meat as though the food had come from heaven itself.

"We should eat some of the meat and then put a basket of meat in the hole in the ground where it is nice and cold for the meat in the next room," Anna said. They all rested on their chairs. Anna fell asleep. She was in a deep sleep. Her breathing was heavy, but she was all right. She had not been able to sleep for nights. Since the war, Anna had slept with one eye open. Today, she was happy, and she had eaten a full meal. She was sleeping soundly for one night. Joseph always got up in the middle of the night. He listened carefully to hear any noises about, and on the sides of the bunker, and above the ground. There was light in the bunker even though it was under the ground. If the hatch was open to the bunker, the light from the sky would come in. Sometimes the family could see the brightness of the sun shining through the branches of pine trees that covered up the hatch. It was almost as though the sun was shining directly at them at that moment. It felt good to see the sun shining. It meant hope for the family. Anna told her family that when the sun is shining into your home, it is as though G-d's light is shining upon you. The bunker hatch was closed most of the time. On an occasion when they felt safe, they would leave the hatch open, but they were all mindful of the Nazis. It was dark under the ground, but somehow a little bit of light from the hatch door always filtered in. It was that small, tiny light that provided the biggest ray of sunshine for their thoughts of hope. Anna expressed the small ray of light as the most powerful ray of sunshine of all the rays, because the light was filtering in from the darkness outside. The light was special. Anna clung to any type of sign from G-d that she and her family would survive this onslaught. She hoped. She prayed. She slept soundly now. Her family slept soundly now. They were more at peace on this night than most of many nights. The help that they received from the church-going villagers and from the Priest and the food that they received was nourishing to their souls too. The sounds of war had stopped. The hope that they would never again hear the sounds of war was on their minds constantly. There were many lights, rays of sunshine that lighted up their lives.

It was a new day. The air was clear. It was not an overly sunny winter day, but the sun did shine a little bit. There was a small wisp-shaped cloud, a wisp of a cirrus cloud in the long, infinitely extended light sky blue clear sky. Anna had woken up early. She awoke with a start. She asked herself the question, "How could she ever forsake her family by falling asleep and not watching for the Nazis". Even now that she had been so befriended by the people in the town. The fears of the war were still with her. She could see Joseph almost still but breathing heavy in his chair. He was still sleeping so she put on her tattered boots, put on her moth-eaten light gray coat with the torn mink collar and she put on her green woolen winter hat. She knew she needed some air. She knew that the pressure about the whole rotten war had gotten to her for many months before. She knew that she felt better about the situation, because she saw people from the town coming to help her and her family. She did not feel alone anymore. But still, she reminded herself, the war is still raging in Slovakia. She looked at the sky and prayed to G-d for peace in her country. She yearned to go back to her home. She shook her head back and forth for she did not know if there was a home left for them to go into.

She climbed the rungs of the ladder. This time as she climbed up the eight rungs of the ladder, she found herself holding on the posts with a stronger grip. She asked herself the question, "Am I feeling better about myself?" She realized at this moment that the visit by the three men was so very meaningful. It had given her the hope that she needed to face the war and the prospect of the war not ending too soon. She felt that she was gripping the posts, because she felt new life in her blood, flowing and reaching out to the tips of her fingers. She climbed up the fastened, steady rungs of the ladder. They seemed to go higher for she felt that there were more rungs to the ladder. "Oh, well," she said to herself as she climbed out of the bunker while placing each foot on the softened ground around the hole of the opening of the bunker. She smiled as she said to herself, "Must have drunk too much wine", and she smiled and then laughed. It was morning, and it was good for her to breath in and out the fresh air of the morning. She felt at peace, and she had not felt this way for many months.

Her mind wandered as she almost fell asleep. She started to think about the Christmas's that she had known before the war. Her street had mostly Jewish people living on it, but the street next to hers had Christian people living in the houses. On Christmas time, Anna's father would always deliver seltzer water and leave the bottles beside the front door of their homes. Every Christmas, the Christians would go to church. The bells on the tower of the church would chime and ring and clang. Everyone regardless of whatever their religious beliefs heard the church bells ringing. The bells' chiming was a call to all men to come and to worship. The call was strong and it was personal, and Anna admitted many times to herself that she would love to go into the church on that Christmas night and feel the warmth of the presence of people worshipping to G-d. Christian friends always told her that the alter in the church was more splendid than any other day in the church. The Priests showed feelings for the Christmas holiday that portrayed to the people that their religion was sincere, rich in thoughts, and reflective of deep thoughts. The people believed in their religion and they wanted to show G-d that they could do good. Anna always respected the Christian religion. Anna always thought that her Christian friends respected her religion.

Anna was suddenly startled by the wild call of a bird overhead. Anna shuddered. She brought back her thoughts that were on her mind quickly, though. She asked, "So why did this horrible person Hitler ever be allowed to pit Christians against the Jews? Why G-d, what reason she asked G-d? Her thoughts started to blur and she became sleepy and her shoulders started to hunch up, as though expressing by themselves the answer, "I do not know the answer". Her hands started to numb from the cold and she rubbed her hands together to get more feeling into them.

She gripped herself. She knew that she had to be on the lookout for Nazis. She looked first in the direction that the bird came from. She did not see anyone. She looked again more carefully taking her time to look for anything that was moving in the distance. She looked to the East and saw no one. She looked to the North and saw no one. Another bird flew over the trees that she was standing next too. She was perplexed at first, but then she calmed down because she did not hear anything—there were no sounds of people walking in the snow or sliding on the ice. She felt a little uneasy, but she knew not to panic. She reassured herself. "I did not see anyone and that is that", she said. She felt her inner strength returning. She thought again of the three men who brought her and her family food. She decided to pray for the war to end. She knew that she had to reach out to G-d and then she would have the hope that she needed to sustain her mind and to help her family. She prayed as she reached out her hands to the sky:

"O Lord, our God, favor Your people Israel;
Accept with love Israel's offering of prayer;
May our worship be ever acceptable to You."

Anna put down her hands. She shook her head back and then forth frontwards. She breathed in the clear air and saw the vapor of her breath. Another bird flew over the trees. She stepped backwards a few paces. She looked over the trees to find the direction in which the bird was flying. She stepped backwards a few more paces. She looked where someone would come through the trees and she saw a small figure moving forward. It looked like the figure was coming towards her. She closed her eyes and breathed in and out a few times. She knew that she had to stand her ground. She had to be brave, and strong, and she had to protect her family. Could it be? She asked herself again, "could it be the delivery man with food?" "Yes", she said to herself. It must be the delivery man". She said to herself, "Just in case it is not the delivery, I will alert the family". She walked over to the hatch and made sure that the hatch was secured, locked shut, and she tapped the bunker to alert her family that she knew that someone was coming". She knew that she had alerted her family so she felt better. She went back to the place near the trees. She waited. The hatch opened. Sam came out of the bunker to help her and secured the hatch. He covered the hatch up with more branches and tore off some branches from pine trees and placed them on the top of the hatch. He sprinkled some snow on the top of the brush and no one would ever know that a bunker was underneath the brush. Sam walked over to his mother. He asked her, "Mom, are you okay?" She answered him with wide-open eyes and admired how tall he stood". She answered, "Oh, Sam, I am all right". Sam asked her, "Is someone coming over here". She answered, "yes", immediately. He asked her, "From where is someone coming?" She answered her son, "Look over there through the trees and you will see someone coming towards us". Sam looked. He watched the man carefully. He said to Anna, "He could be the delivery man". He paused. "Just in case", he said, "I should stand behind some of the trees where the man cannot see me". Anna agreed. She said, "It is always wise to be cautious".

The man continued to trek through the woods. At times it seemed as though he was going faster and faster. He never looked behind him, though. He must have looked sideways to see if there were any Nazis in the woods. He must have been listening for the sounds of war for every once in a while the sound of the shooting started up. There was always no way to know when the sound would stop. The man who was coming through the woods was coming closer and closer. Anna waited, but she waited with some feelings of trepidation for the fear was real. She kept looking for Sam who was well-hidden on the side of a tree. He had a large ax in one hand. He had found the ax on the side of one of the trees weeks and weeks ago and had decided to hide the ax under some brush. He was ready to fight just in case he needed to do so. He was a man now. He was tall and although lanky from the lack of food at times, he was nevertheless strong enough to fight. He knew how to fight now. He was no longer the weakling who went to school and came back home in the afternoon. He had asked one of the partisans who had stopped near the bunker to teach him some tricks. Sam was prepared to fight. So were his brothers. His sister refused to fight. His mother and his father had learned how to fight. Sam was thinking, "At least they would not go down without a good fight".

The lone figure appeared. He came out of the woods. He saw Anna. He waved his hand as if to say hello. Anna waved back. Sam stood silently behind the tree. There was no verbal exchange between any of them.

The ice crackled underneath the lone man's feet. His feet had been going that quickly. His body almost resisted the motion of his stopping as it appeared as though his feet wanted to move forward. "Yes". He said. I have come to deliver food to you, Anna. He introduced himself as Franz. Anna shivered for a moment, but then she relaxed. She would not dare look towards Sam. "So what have you brought us for this time?" Anna asked. The man smiled and said, "I have brought you Christmas cakes that are filled with dried fruits and nuts. I know that you will like these cakes. I had someone at the village bake these cakes for you". Anna just smiled and said, "Oh". "Yes" Franz continued. "There is a large salami and a lot of sugar cookies in my knapsack and he took off the knapsack and opened it up. Anna exclaimed, as she gently reached into the knapsack and pulled out the cakes, laid them down on the cold ground, and reached in for the salami, and then she pulled out the bag of cookies. Anna was happy, and she breathed in and out, and wobbled for a minute or so from one leg to the other. She said, as she quietly toned down her wonder and feelings of enthusiasm, "I thank you so much and please say 'hello' to our friend the foreman and tell him that Anna and her family said to say, "Thank you and to wish him and his family a very merry Christmas. "Yes", the man said, and he wrapped up the knapsack and placed it back on his back as he reached and stretched for the handles on the knapsack. Anna wanted him to stay for a minute longer. She said, "Is there any news about the war". "Oh, yes," was the lone man's answer. "So what is happening?" prompted Anna. "The war is raging in Hungary", he said. "But", Anna said, "what about here in Slovakia?" And she poised and asked the question as the words came from her mouth very slowly, "Are the Nazis still taking Jews to the camps?" The man had an expression of earnest caring on his face and he answered, "the Russians are winning in Russia and the word is that their armies are moving straight for Slovakia to liberate the Slovakian people. "Oh", Anna exclaimed as she clapped her hands. The man smiled and said, "I am happy that I can bring you some food". Anna asked, "When will the next delivery be?" "Oh", the man replied, "I will try to make it in another week. But the weather may hold me back". Anna said, "If the weather holds you back, then I understand". The man smiled and said, "Well, I had best be going". Anna asked, "Will it take you long to get home?" Not too long. "I only live outside of Micholovce." "So", Anna asked, "Will you cut through the trees?" "I could go any which way, but going through the trees seems safer". "I know better than to go back the same way that I came, though." Anna asked, "And you are not afraid of the Nazis?" Everyone is afraid of the Nazis, but you cannot fear the Nazis. You have to evade them. You have to do this or meet them head on. That is what the Russians are doing. The Russians are giving the Germans a good beating. "Finally. Anna", the man said, "I will see you in about a week. We will live to see the end of the war". Anna had tears in her eyes, "Yes, we will see you soon, and we will live to see the end of the war". Anna thought to herself as she saw the man tie his shawl around his neck, and turn around, and head for the woods. There were no good-byes. No one said goodbye these day. His visit helped Anna to recover from any doubts that she may have had. Also, the visit by the three men came right at the right time for Anna. Anna was fearful that she was losing her strength to go on. When she saw the three men, her spirit for living was renewed. She knew that there was goodness in the world despite the ugly war. She needed to know this.

The war did drag on, but it was less intense in Micholovce than in other surrounding areas and countries. The delivery of the food to Anna and her family continued until they left the bunker that they had called their home.

In the remaining months that followed the Christmas of 1944, Anna and her family felt their spirit in living and in coping with the war renewed. They made plans. They made plans for leaving the bunker and traveling through the woods. They knew that they would find their way back. They wondered if they could find their home in tact. There was so much bombing. They wondered many times how many homes were destroyed by the bombs. They wondered if their temple where they worshipped was still standing. Most of all they wondered how many people were left? How many people would come home to Micholovce was always a big question that loomed on their minds. From the reports given by visiting Partisans, they knew that other people were hiding in the woods. There was hope.

Word came from a villager on one quiet day. The villager found them and announced that the war was over. Anna and Joseph were going to leave the bunker soon anyway. Anna and Joseph had decided to try to go back to Micholovce. There had not been any stifling, stark-sounding noises of war tanks and war armament so they assumed by themselves that the war had ended. Joseph told Anna to be cautious and not to be hasty about leaving the bunker, though. Anna was set on returning to her home, but she listened to Joseph.

The day had finally come to leave the bunker. It was a clear day and the sky was a lighter blue than usual, and it was a memorable day in May. Some of the snow from the winter was still frozen solid in spots along the trail. But the season's new growth of wild grasses had begun to glow with their natural shade of green colors. Birds had flown out of their nests and encircled the area and returned to their nests chirping with their newborn hatchlings. Birds were no longer making their gawking sounds. A large size bird circled the wooded trees near where the bunker was. He perched for a moment on one of the strong arms of the branches on one of the mighty trees. He pecked at some of the leaves on the trees. He flew from the branch with the twig of leaves in his mouth. He circled wider and wider around the trees near the bunker. He flew high up into the sky, but then descended and flew directly over Anna and Joseph. The bird dropped the small branch out of its mouth and the branch fell and it landed on the ground near Anna and Joseph. Joseph picked it up and put the branch in his pocket. He told Anna, "This is a keepsake for us to take with us". Anna smiled and breathed in the fresh air. She said to Joseph, "It is a beautiful day". She paused and said softly, "Favor me oh Lord, and I will move mountains". Joseph held her hand. They walked down the trail. Sam followed. Martin came next. Bernard walked behind Martin. Henry followed Bernard. Edith followed Henry.

Cheryl Freier

Cheryl Freier

Printed in the United States
By Bookmasters